THE HOLY SPIRIT,
YOUR RETREAT DIRECTOR

A Manual for a Dir
Based on the Ignatia

by

Aloysius J. Owen, S.J.

ALBA · HOUSE   NEW · YORK

SOCIETY OF ST. PAUL, 2187 VICTORY BLVD., STATEN ISLAND, NEW YORK 10314

269
O 93

Library of Congress Cataloging in Publication Data

Owen, Aloysius J
  The Holy Spirit, your retreat director.

  Work is based on the Spiritual exercises of St. Ignatius.
    1. Retreats   2. Loyola, Ignacio de, Saint,
1491-1556. Exercitia spiritualia. I. Loyola, Ignacio de, Saint,
1491-1556. Exercitia spiritualia. II. Title.
BX2375.A3093   269'.6   79-14945
ISBN: 0-8189-0387-2

Nihil Obstat:
Daniel V. Flynn, J.C.D.

Imprimatur:
Joseph T. O'Keefe
Vicar General, Archdiocese of New York
April 24, 1979

Designed, printed and bound in the United States of
America by the Fathers and Brothers of the
Society of St. Paul, 2187 Victory Boulevard,
Staten Island, New York, 10314, as part of their
communications apostolate.

1 2 3 4 5 6 7 8 9 (Current Printing: first digit).

CONTENTS

INTRODUCTION

This work on the Spiritual Exercises of St. Ignatius might have been entitled *A Word of God That You May Know God* because I shall primarily direct myself *to you*, a prospective "active" retreatant (not to retreat directors). And so begin already at this point by actively praying:

> *Almighty God, Father of our Lord Jesus Christ, faith in your word is the way to wisdom, and to ponder your divine plan is to grow in truth. Open my eyes to your deeds, my ears to the sound of your call, so that every act increases my sharing in the life you have offered me. Grant this through your Son, Christ our Lord and your Holy Spirit.*
>
> *Father, you gave the human race eternal salvation through the motherhood of the Virgin Mary. May I experience the help of her prayers in my life for through her I received the very source of life, your Son, our Lord Jesus Christ.*

Ponder with Mary:

> *In the beginning was the Word; the Word was in God's presence, and the Word was God. . . . The Word became flesh and made his dwelling among us, and we have seen his glory; the glory of an only Son coming from the Father, filled with enduring love* (Jn 1:14).

I call to your attention that this is to be a prayerful retreat which I am inviting you to make. So to initiate your renewed life of prayer, I shall

quote prayers and excerpts from the Bible appropriate to the topics treated. As you read, *stop, pray and ponder the message of the Holy Spirit!*

A Word of God to Know God

When you make your retreat, through the Word of God, you will come to know God, the Holy Trinity and the Three Divine Persons. You will come to know the Father—Life. "You are created to praise, reverence and serve God, our Lord, and by this means to save your soul," that is, receive the new life principle, sanctifying grace. You will come to know the Son—Light. St. Ignatius intends his Exercises to give you an illumination, "an intimate knowledge of our Lord, that you may love him more and follow him more closely." And you will come to know the Holy Spirit—Love, "that you may in all things love and serve the Divine Majesty."

Pray:

God, you open the way to your heavenly kingdom for those born of water and the Holy Spirit. Increase your grace in your servant that I may be cleansed from my sins and through your love attain what you have promised. "Your word, Lord is truth; make us holy in the truth" (Jn 17:7).

This divine pattern permeates the *Spiritual Exercises.* Everything that you do on your retreat will help you to understand and personally experience the effects of this divine concern and love God has for you. With the help of the Holy Spirit, and Mary's intercession—ever to Christ through Mary—under the guidance of your director, you will see exemplified in God's word, the Old and New Testaments, how God proclaims the Good Tidings. You will see this divine pattern carried out in Christ's Mystical Body, the Church. May you see this clearly, humbly and obediently in the way Vatican II attests to the divine action in men and in the world.

You, as a member of that Mystical Body, are *an active participant*, not a spectator, in the drama of salvation!

Pray:

> *God of wisdom and truth, without you there is no wisdom or truth. Protect your Church. Grant her unity and ineffable joy in you. "If you stay in my word, you will be my disciples, and you will know the truth, says the Lord"* (Jn 8:31-32).

The Meaning of the Word of God

The *New American Bible* gives the following definition: "The term 'word of God' is used in more than one sense in the Bible: A message of God to men; the communications of God; the plan of God for man's salvation; the power of God as Creator of the universe; the Gospel of Christ and the actual words spoken by Christ. Scripture is often referred to as 'word of God' because it is his revelation. But the most important use of the phrase 'Word of God' is as a *proper name for Jesus*, the Son of God. Jesus was the Word for all eternity and the Word was God. The Word was made flesh and lived in our midst as God-Man. The Word is living and is the source of all life for men. The Word is the victorious King and Ruler of the universe in the final phase of the world."

Communication and Encounter with the Word of God

When you make your retreat you will be "communicating" with God. So, as St. Ignatius advises, during your retreat pass the time in an atmosphere of tranquil prayer, silence and seclusion *listening* to God speaking.

Pray:

> *God of light and splendor of the truth, lead me on the way of salvation according to your promises, that I may wholeheartedly accept the words of life and forever cling to the Word of truth. "For upright is the word of the Lord; and all his works are trustworthy. He loves justice and right; of the kindness of the Lord the earth is full"* (Ps 33:4-5).

St. Ignatius says "In this seclusion the mind is not engaged in many things, but can give its whole attention to one single interest, that is, to the service of its Creator and its spiritual progress."

Your retreat will open the way to encounter the Word of God, to bring you closer to Christ. In the words of Scripture which are presented to you for meditation and contemplation, you are told the Good News of salvation. But to have such an encounter with the Word, you must have faith, acceptance, recognition and response to God's invitation to listen to his words and come to him. On opening your heart to God who speaks to you while you are making your retreat, your mind will be filled and directed by his Holy Spirit, and you will find yourself in his presence, a recipient of that supreme gift of Life, Light and Love.

Pray:

> *Father, may I be filled with the new light by the coming of the Word to me. May the light of faith shine in all my words and actions. "The revelation of your words sheds light, giving understanding to the simple"* (Ps 119).

Before giving the advice quoted above St. Ignatius says: "If in order to serve and praise God our Lord one withdraws from friends and acquaintances and from many occupations that were not undertaken with a pure intention, he gains no little merit before the Divine Majesty. Ordinarily, the progress made in the Exercises will be greater, the more the exercitant withdraws from all friends and acquaintances and from all wordly cares" (Ex 20). You may reflect on this advice and try, during the retreat, to make the visit of your dearest Friend, Jesus, as pleasant as possible. Turn off the radio and the television, no more house work, sit down and listen to him as did Mary Magdalene who chose the better part!

The most important task you have during your retreat is to *listen*. You are in the presence of the Lord so let yourself be filled with the very thought. Listen! It is God who is speaking, who calls you. It is Christ who is visiting you and he comes bearing those precious gifts of Life, Light and Love. Place yourself in the proper disposition to choose what God wishes of you, accept his plan of salvation and conform yourself to it.

While you are making your retreat, "the Word of God" in the Bible gives you a greater knowledge of God. The prophets of the Old Testament foretell that man will be given a new heart and a new spirit. This is why you make a retreat. You will have the law written afresh in your heart. As St. Theresa of Avila says, "you will not merely know but *savor* the fruits of the Spirit."

The New Testament, especially St. John, will teach you the pathway to knowledge, that you are to "remain" in the Word of Christ, and the Word of truth is to remain in you. The Word of Christ is to be infused into your heart under the influx of the Spirit, to transform you. This Word, having penetrated, is what St. John calls the living water, the ointment, the seed sown by God. Your retreat will be the moment when the seed sown will hopefully fall on fertile soil!

> *The seed is the word of God, Christ is the sower. All who come to him will live forever* (Mt 13:37).

May you, out of love and loyalty to him, become a true disciple of Jesus, that is, live docilely with Christ, his Word, live in the fullness of faith, so that "you may know Christ more clearly, love him more dearly and follow him more nearly."

St. John tells us that if we love Christ we will love others. "This, remember is the message from the beginning: we should love one another. . . . I ask you, how can God's love survive in a man who has enough of this world's goods yet closes his heart to his brother when he sees him in need. Little children, let us love in deed and in truth and not merely talk about it. This is our way of knowing we are committed to the truth and are at peace before him no matter what our consciences charge us with; for God is greater than our hearts and all is known to him" (1Jn 3:11, 17-21).

Pray:

> *Father, I want to be strong enough to love you above all and my brothers and sisters because of you. Fill me with the power of your unbounded love.*

Imitation of the Word of God

The New Testament on speaking of your obligations to love your neighbor asks: "If you do not love your neighbor whom you can see, how can you love God whom you cannot see?" This is why the Second Person, the Word, became man. St. Ignatius urges you to imitate Christ. He tells you: "This is to ask for what I desire. Here it will be to ask for an intimate knowledge of our Lord, who has become man for me, that I may love him more and follow him more closely."

Pray:

> *Father, keep before me the wisdom and love you have revealed in your Son. Help me to be like him in word and deed. "Your word is a lamp for my feet, and a light for my path"* (Pss 105,119).

Father Goncalves da Camara (who "spied" on Ignatius at the Professed house in Rome) tells us: "Just as our Father, who observed all the rules of the Spiritual Exercises in all his actions, had them planted in his soul and all his actions sprang from them" had the same attitude toward the *Following of Christ* by Thomas a Kempis. Father da Camara says: "Conversing with Father Ignatius is like reading it in action!" So, I urge you to read it during your retreat and even after your retreat!

In his *Spiritual Exercises* St. Ignatius makes Christ the center, the model of our spirituality. In your retreat you will endeavor and be helped to acquire an exact view of Christ so that you will become like him, another Christ and thus arrive at a radical conversion and an ever more total surrender of self.

Greater Awareness of God's Presence

Such awareness will be brought about by such imitation of Christ.

Pray:

> *Father, help me to be like Christ your Son, who loved the world and died for our salvation. Inspire me by his love and guide me by his example. "Your words, Lord, are spirit and life. You have the words of everlasting life"* (Jn 6:64,69).

I recall the story of the little girl being taught to spell by an extreme Marxist teacher. He told her to write on the blackboard: "God is nowhere." The little girl wrote: "God is now here."

Incidentally, I suggest you do not listen to and be deceived by the so-called "social justice" advocated by Marxists and even absurdly self-designated Christian Marxists! For wherever the Communists have taken over the very existence of God is denied and children are forbidden to be taught that he exists!

Here is how St. Ignatius lived in God's presence—and do not forget he was a very busy man, fully occupied in founding the Society of Jesus. Da Camara tells us: "Whatever our Father does for God, he does it with admirable recollection and promptitude. It seems he not only envisions God present before him but actually sees him with his eyes."

I quote St. Ignatius again: "The more the soul is in solitude and seclusion the more fit it is to approach and be united with him, the more it disposes itself to receive graces and gifts from the infinite goodness of its God."

Pray:

> *God, Creator and Ruler of all things, be mindful of us. Make us feel your presence so that we may serve you alone.*

Listen to God's Word

You may have heard of the definition of a good conversationalist: "one who does not interrupt me when I'm speaking." This is also true of prayer, even in meditation and contemplation. So, you should imitate Mary who *pondered in her heart* what happened. Also, be like Mary, Martha's sister who sat at Christ's feet and *listened!*

Now this does not mean emptying the mind! If an idle mind is the devil's workshop, what is an empty mind? Rather, after you have opened up your heart, your mind, your spirit to his Holy Spirit and welcomed him, fill your whole being with awareness of God's presence and, when you hear him speak, listen! Then, inspired by what he suggests, speak with him about your temporal concerns. In fact, when you really do listen, he will suggest what should concern you most, will enlighten you to see this in the light of his will and of his love. He will advise you, too, no matter what is happening: *Be concerned*, but *never anxious*!

Love of Solitude and Silence

"It is in silence and repose that the devout Christian makes progress and learns the hidden truths of Scripture. Night after night, he finds tears shed for washing and cleansing his soul. He will find waiting in his cell (your solitude and silence) what he has so often sought in vain outside of it. If he therefore withdraws himself from his acquaintances and friends, God will be near to him with his holy Angels" (*The Following of Christ* Bk I, Ch. 6).

Love and Loyalty to the Church, Christ's Mystical Body

Before you go on retreat I recommend that you read over prayerfully Pius XII's *Mystici Corporis*, the encyclical letter on the Mystical Body of Christ. I quote from the introduction:

"We first learned of the Mystical Body of Christ, which is the Church (Col 1:24), from the lips of the Redeemer himself. Illustrating, as it does, the grand and inestimable privilege of our intimate union with a Head so exalted, this doctrine is certainly calculated by its sublime dignity to draw all spiritual-minded men to deep and serious study, and to give them in the truths which it unfolds to the mind, a strong incentive to such virtuous conduct as is conformable to its lessons. This is why we have thought it fitting to speak with you on this subject through this *Encyclical Letter*, examining and explaining above all what concerns the Church

Militant. The surpassing magnificence of the argument attracts Us; the circumstances of the present hour urges Us on."

In the light of the last phrase, pray:

> *Lord, you are true and faithful, and you fulfill what you promise. Look upon your Church. Keep her in faith throughout the ages and make her a shining light in the darkness of the world through your Word. "Even now I find my joy in the suffering I endure for you. In my own flesh I fill up what is lacking in the sufferings of Christ for the sake of his body, the church"* (Col 1:24).

You will realize more and more during your retreat that your Holy Mother the Church is Christ's Mystical Body living and suffering in the world today. "One flock and one Shepherd," the shepherd, the successor of St. Peter, the Vicar of Christ on earth, the Holy Father.

When Christ asked Peter if he too would leave him, Peter cried out: "Lord, to whom shall I go? Thou alone hast the words of eternal life!" Some unfaithful followers deserted Jesus as so many are doing today led by the signs of the devil.

Pride and Confusion

I exhort you to make the same reply to the Holy Father as did Peter to Christ, should you be tempted by false shepherds to reject the authority of the Church and of the Holy Father. During your retreat I urge you to read over prayerfully and carefully St. Ignatius' *Rules for thinking with the Church*, rules so needed today!

Pray:

> *Lord, guide the course of world events and give your Church the joy and peace of serving you in freedom. "The Spirit of the Lord fills the whole world. It holds all things together and knows every word spoken by man"* (Wi 1:7).

Just as when Jesus Christ first came down to earth centuries ago he was unknown to the world, rejected by his own, so today he is in the world. So many of his own not only do not know him but whole nations are being subjected in the name of "social justice" to Marxist atheism. They reject Christ today in his Mystical Body, the Church. Listen to what St. Ignatius would say to those who desert and betray him and lead their flocks astray: "*We must put aside all judgment of our own*, and keep the mind ever ready to *obey* in all things the true Spouse of Christ, our Holy Mother, the *hierarchical* (authoritative) Church."

There are some who would say that this is typical of a person of those days of reaction, legalism, authoritarianism, days of primacy, the dictatorship of the hierarchical Church versus the People of God. In order to strengthen your love and loyalty and for making it more like that of *Loyola* I quote this passage from Vatican II: "For, by this sense of faith which is aroused and sustained by the Spirit of Truth, God's People accept not the word of men but the very Word of God. It clings without fail to the faith delivered to the saints, penetrates it more deeply by accurate insights, and applies it more thoroughly to life. *All this it does under the lead of a sacred teaching authority to which it loyally defers" (Lumen Gentium, 12).*

Pray:

> *Father, let the gift of life continue to grow in me, drawing me from death to faith, hope and love. Keep me alive in Jesus Christ, watchful in prayer and true to his teaching till your glory is revealed in me.*

Jesus said: "I solemnly assure you, if a man is true to my word he shall never see death" (Jn 8:5).

Therefore, during your retreat ask the Holy Spirit to give you Ignatian love and loyalty to his Church. Ask especially for the gift of *balance*. For example, when a question of change versus stability comes up, think of a tree. It changes every season but it must be firmly rooted! An instance may be found in dogmatic terminology, the use of the term "transubstantiation." Due to the neglect of scholastic philosophy today this term may be confusing if not unintelligible. So, change the terminology but do not deny the substance: the *Real*

Let us pray:

> *O Lord, grant that we may enjoy the eternal presence of your Word, which is foreshadowed by our earthly reception of your precious Body and Blood.*

Further, when there is disagreement with authority, the attitude of the true Christian is quite different from that of the rebel, who in the words of Satan, "will not serve." He turns away and goes into opposition out of pride. The true Christian, if he sees that, for the moment there is no solution, awaits a more propitious time, accepts the situation and does everything he can in his own circumstances to reach a solution in fidelity to the word of God as found in the Church, the Mystical Body of Christ. But he keeps "family business to himself" and does not call on the media of communications—press, radio and TV— to express his views in opposition to the teachings of the Church!

Pray:

> *All-powerful Father, you have built your Church on the rock of St. Peter's confession of faith. May nothing divide or weaken our unity in faith and love. "Blessed are they who hear the word of God and keep it"* (Lk 11:25).

The Theology of the Spiritual Exercises

Etymologically the term "theology" comes from the Greek *theos* and *logos* (God and word). As expressed in the words *A Word of God that you may know God*, your retreat will be theological. Of course, it will not be a course in theology so at the end you will not get a degree. Yet, according to your God-given talents, you will appreciate in varying degrees the Word of God as found in the Exercises. You will receive the ultimate fruit of them as expressed in the final exercise: *The Contemplation to attain the Love of God*, "The intimate knowledge of the many blessings received."

By "intimate knowledge" St. Ignatius means "knowing everything in its innermost reality as a reflection of God's image." During your retreat you will come to know, in the light of the Holy

Spirit, what God intends you to do for him. After you have pondered "with great affection how much God our Lord has done for you and how much he has given you of what he possesses" (Ex. 232), you cannot help but make yourself another Christ for the world, or, as St. Ignatius says: "In all things love and serve the Divine Majesty" (Ex. 233).

You will see that what the theology of the Exercises will set before you is of the kind that *places you before* divine revelation to perceive of what you are capable. It will help you reflect on the meaning of the divine manifestation expressed in Sacred Scripture. But, above all, it will help you appreciate all the means God has put at your disposal to utilize them to his greater glory: *ad majorem Dei gloriam. The teacher of this theology will be the Holy Spirit*, who will give you this course in five lessons.

Your first lesson will be a *review* of the knowledge you had prior to the retreat. This frequently has to be repeated while making it.

Your second lesson will be your *personal perception* of the Exercises. This is to learn the relationship of theological realities to your own way of life which is to be inserted into God's design.

Your third lesson will be *enlightenment as to the meaning* of your own life in relation to the realization of God's eternal plan. Your personal history enters into the framework of the theology of history. You see, in the light of the Spirit, how Christ continues acting through you and how you can be the continuation of Christ.

Your fourth lesson will be a *progressive integration.* You must gradually go out of yourself and enter into God. You no longer see yourself as the center but as in orbit around God, the Eternal Now.

Your fifth lesson will be *unification*, oneness in Christ. When your inner vision is transformed in this way, you discover in the Gospel the permanent way of Christ, the way to imitate him so as to become the Christ of today. What Christ did two thousand years ago, the glorified Christ now does in you through his Spirit present within you. There is that "living in Christ," that deeper unification and integration of your being in Christ. Thus God makes you "die to the old man" with Christ and rise again with him in a newness of life and an increase of service. Christ is true "Salvation."

Pray:

> *God, you took note of man's fall and redeemed him by the coming of your only Son. Grant that I who profess this incarnation with humble devotion may share also in the fruits of his redemption. "Shine on the world like bright stars; you are offering it the word of life"* (Ph 2:15-16).

By the end of this "course" your Teacher, the Holy Spirit, will have made you realize that your perception of the conditions of the world, your knowledge of your own qualifications and potentialities are to be seen, not only in a sociological context but also as part of his work in you. I also call to your mind that you are taking this "course" under the guidance of Holy Mother the Church. You must ever keep in mind that you are a member of the Church, a member of Christ's Mystical Body, the Church, the means established by Christ for communicating grace; for saving souls.

Pray:

> *Lord, grant that world events may take place in peace according to your Word. May your Church enjoy peacefulness in her service to you. "Happy are they who have kept the word with a generous heart and yield a harvest through perseverance"* (Lk 8:1-5).

The Spiritual Exercises and the History of Salvation

> *Father in heaven, the loving plan of your wisdom took flesh in Jesus Christ and changed mankind's history by his command of perfect love. May our fulfillment of his command reflect your wisdom and bring salvation to the ends of the earth. "Glorify the Lord. He sends forth his command to the earth, swiftly runs his word"* (Ps 147:45).

The retreat I hope you will make may be said to be your encounter with the Word of God as an integral part of the history of salvation of which you are a part. By the history of salvation you are to understand the entire history of the Church—of mankind—saved from the beginning of time—Alpha—to the end of time—Omega. You will learn to share in this history of grace, especially by finding your place in the Church and in mankind. So that you will be inspired by the Holy Spirit to put yourself at the disposition of God's design of love, for the Holy Spirit is Love!

What is the meaning of salvific history? It means that salvation is offered *in time*. It takes place in a series of acts which you must vitally and interiorly share. These acts are substantially those presented in the preaching of the first Christian community, in the Apostles Creed etc. Participation in these acts is achieved through the sacraments and other "exercises" of Christian life.

Salvific history also means that salvation is offered according to a temporal succession, not at an indivisible moment. It always follows a progression which comprises successive and privileged times. Vatican II expresses it thus: "In carefully planning and preparing the salvation of the human race, the God of supreme love, by a special dispensation, chose for himself a people to whom he might entrust his promise. . . . The principal purpose to which the plan of the Old Testament was directed is to prepare for the coming both of Christ, the universal Redeemer, and of the messianic kingdom, to announce this coming by prophecy and to indicate its meaning through various types" (*Verbum Dei 14-16*). There is presupposed a hierarchy of salvific events and moments linked together, among which some are outstanding.

Pray:

> *Father, all powerful God, your eternal Word took flesh on our earth when the Virgin Mary placed her life at the service of your plan. Lift up my mind in watchful hope to hear the voice which announces his glory. "The Word of God is living and active; it probes the thoughts and motives of our hearts"* (Heb 4:12).

Salvation is the profound meaning of history, it's "truth." Vatican II says: "Therefore, since everything asserted by the inspired writers must be held to be asserted by the Holy Spirit, it follows that the books of Scripture must be acknowledged as teaching firmly, faithfully and without error that truth which God wanted put into the sacred writing for the sake of our salvation" (*Verbum Dei, 11*).

St. Ignatius makes clear that salvation is the purpose of history, or your life as part of that history. In his definition of "Spiritual Exercises" he says: "We call Spiritual Exercises every way of preparing and disposing the soul to rid itself of all inordinate attachments, and, after their removal, of *seeking and finding the will of God* in the disposition of our life for the salvation of souls" (Ex. 1).

History acquires its specific value from the salvific end it imports and by which it will be judged. The eschatological dimension is therefore necessary for a correct appreciation of salvation offered in history.

Pray:

> *Come, Holy Spirit, Creator blessed and in our hearts take up thy rest. Come with thy grace and heavenly aid to fill the hearts which thou hast made.*
>
> *Lord, you saved me. As a child of light, I long to be your faithful witness before my brothers today. Make me a follower of the Light and a doer of the Truth.*
>
> *"Jesus looked up to heaven and prayed: O Father most holy, consecrate them by means of truth—Your word is truth"* (Jn 17:17).
>
> *Holy Mary, Mother of God, pray for us sinners now and at the hour of our death.*
>
> *Blest are you among women and blest is the fruit of your womb. "But who am I that the mother of my Lord should come to me?"* (Lk 1:42-43).

LIBER SAPIENTIÆ

VERITAS

Chapter 1

AN "ACTIVE" IGNATIAN RETREAT

I invite you to consider prayerfully whether you will make a retreat and prior thereto will consider what kind of a retreat it will be. Of course, there are all sorts of retreats: directed retreats, group retreats, communitarian retreats—a real Heinz's variety! This is quite in keeping with St. Ignatius' adaptability: "According to circumstances of time, place and person." So, there must be adaptation to the needs of the retreatant, that is, the method is to be *suited to you rather than you to the method.*

Pray:

> *Your light is true light, Lord, and your Truth shines like the day. Direct me to salvation through your life-giving words. May I be saved always embracing your Light.*

The Retreat Adjusted to You the Retreatant

Although St. Ignatius' work, the *Spiritual Exercises*, is available and I trust you will obtain a copy before you decide to make an Ignatian retreat, I shall nonetheless quote from the text occasionally. Here is a very pertinent passage from what are known as the *Introductory Observations.*

"The Spiritual Exercises must be *adapted* to the condition of the one who is to engage in them, that is, to his age, education and talent. Thus exercises that he could not easily bear, or from which he would derive no profit, should not be given to one without education or with little natural ability.

"Similarly, each one should be given those exercises that would be more helpful and profitable according to the degree of progress he wishes to attain" (Ex. 10).

I said above that the method is to be suited to you. In keeping with this there are many varieties of Exercises based on your purpose and your abilities. Instead of quoting from the text I refer you to the *Introductory Observations* 18 and 19.

From the former you will see that St. Ignatius intended to base the type of retreat you will make on your purpose: that you may receive the grace to live as a child of God, Brother of Christ; or that you may receive the grace of a greater commitment, in the light of vocation, a call of Christ; and no matter what the state of life, the grace of renewal, enlightenment, advance in your spiritual life and of greater apostolicity, making Christ known to all with whom you come in contact in your daily life.

He proposes religious instruction as to the spiritual life and its practice, especially the examination of conscience, confession, prayer, meditation and the sacrament with a view to amendment of life, devotion to Christ and his Blessed Mother. the Holy Spirit and to the Father. So, pray—note I do not say recite— *the Our Father, the Hail Mary, the Glory be to the Father, the Son and the Holy Spirit.*

Today more and more are choosing to make retreats according to the *Nineteenth Introductory Observation.* This method brings God more intimately into your daily life. You do not go entirely apart from your daily life yet at the same time you make God more and more present to you and to those with whom you have daily contact, your family, your friends, neighbors, fellow workers. After you have made such a retreat I am sure you will find his presence nearer and nearer.

> *Father, you taught the hearts of your faithful people by sending them the light of your Holy Spirit. In that Holy Spirit give me right judgment and the joy of his comfort and guidance. "The Spirit we have received is not the world's spirit but God's Spirit, helping us to recognize the gifts given*

> *us. We speak not in words of human wisdom but words taught by the Holy Spirit"* (1 Cor 2:12-13).

The Origin of the Directed Retreat

Very appropriately I propose this prayer:

> *God, you raised St. Ignatius in your Church to inspire men to work for your greater glory. Grant that I may labor on earth with his help after his example and merit to be crowned with him in heaven.*

Though the technical term is "directed," I would like to call it also a "direct" retreat for it is not directed to you as a member of a group but *directly to you as an individual.* Some think that this type of "Exercise" is an innovation. This is far from being so. In fact the earliest Ignatian Exercises were directed and the group retreat developed later in France due to the large number of retreatants.

In his *History of the Spiritual Exercises* Father Ignacio Iparraguirre tells us that when St. Ignatius was living at the residence in Rome, even though several persons were making a retreat there, each retreatant made it under the guidance of one of the Jesuits. The retreatant made it as an individual and was known to the Jesuit community as "the invisible guest."

So it is not surprising that many who "give the Exercises,"—that is St. Ignatius' term for director; for him the Holy Spirit was the real Director— think that the directed retreat is most suited for our present day. Even if a "group" is making the retreat, the director only addresses the group, and the fewer the better, once or at most twice a day and more commonly not even once.

Now, I have no intention here to belittle the "group" retreat. I do recall that according to early accounts, when the "group" retreat was introduced the reaction of some "directed" retreat directors was quite similar to that of some "group" retreat directors to the "directed" retreat now. In fact, some of the best retreat directors I know give real Ignatian retreats in this form in keeping with the "adaptability" of St.

Ignatius according to "circumstance of time, place and person."

St. Ignatius did not develop all the elements the "one giving the retreat" should employ. He foresaw that, in the course of time, man's problems would change and theology develop—not substantially as I said before but in application and terminology. So there would be other ways of studying and presenting the Bible, God's Word. That is why he adopted a system which would be valid in other times for men filled with the spirit of the Exercises, who would fashion a theological and biblical interpretation—ever in keeping with his *Rules for thinking with the Church*!

"We must put aside all judgment of our own, and keep the mind ever ready and prompt to obey in all things the true Spouse of Jesus Christ and our Holy Mother, the *hierarchical* Church" (Ex. 353).

In keeping with this Ignatian spirit pray:

> *God, the source of all justice and goodness, you hate wickedness and abhor falsehood. Guide the way of your servants and grant true joy in your Church. "We will devote ourselves to prayer and to the ministry of the word"* (Ac 6:4).

The Spiritual Exercises and Social Justice

Made properly the Spiritual Exercises will show you the real meaning of social justice: *cooperation with Christ* for the salvation of your neighbor. Out of love for God you shall love your neighbor as yourself.

Since St. Ignatius' definition of love will teach you how you are to share in the history of salvation, not only by receiving but by *giving*, I shall quote from his marvelous *Contemplation to attain the love of God*, the acme of the Exercises.

"Love ought to manifest itself in deeds rather than in words. Love consists in mutual sharing of goods, for example, the lover gives and shares with the beloved what he possesses, or something of that which he has or is able to give; and vice versa, the beloved shares with the lover. Hence, if one has knowledge, he shares it with one who does not possess it; and so also if one has honors, or riches. Thus, one always gives to the other" (Ex. 230).

Of course you also know that "you should love your neighbor as yourself for love of God." So you will learn not only how to save your own soul but how you can be, in Christ, with Christ and through Christ, a co-redeemer of others. You will realize too what St. John says is still true even after Christ has come: "He was in the world, and through him the world was made, yet the world did know who he was. To his own he came, yet his own did not accept him" (Jn 10-11).

So, one of the graces you will receive on your retreat will be the desire to bring back into the fold those sheep who have gone astray due to what St. Ignatius calls the marks of Satan. He says: "Imagine you see the chief of all the enemy in the vast plain about Babylon, seated on a great *throne*—Pride—of *fire and smoke*—Confusion, his appearance inspiring horror and terror" (Ex. 140).

But too often this pride infects the shepherds of the flock who reject the "authoritarian" Church and who feed their sheep with the tares of confusion. Out of love for Christ and those of Christ's one flock, under one Shepherd, the Holy Father, those who reject him and his Mystical Body, will come through you to know him more clearly, love him more dearly and follow him more nearly. Thus your whole being will be "theologized" and "apostolized," that is, you will come to know God and make him known to others.

Pray:
> *Christ, eternal Shepherd, look on your flock as it rises from sleep—feed me with the word of life and the bread of heaven. Keep me safe from the wolf—Satan—and hireling—false shepherd—and make me faithful in listening to your voice.*
>
> *Almighty and eternal God, through the coming of your Son you radiated a new light. Grant that I who share in the benefits of his birth from a Virgin may also obtain membership in his kingdom of grace. "Mary treasured all these words and pondered them in her heart"* (Lk 2:19).

You will find out in the light of the Holy Spirit what God intends you to do for him. After you have "pondered" this in your heart imitating Mary (through Mary to Christ) with great affection, you will come to know how much God our Lord has done for you and how much he has given you of what he possesses. He will not be outdone in generosity. You give him yourself, a created, finite being—a pretty small tomato. In return he gives you himself, his constant personal action in you. So, after learning of your "apostolic" mission, you will resolve to become a "prophet" a witness to the reality you have experienced. You cannot, then, help but make yourself another Christ for the world, or, as St. Ignatius says: "In all things love and serve the Divine Majesty."

Today there is a great concern for *social justice.* This is a great gift of God. However, since it is of God it is to be understood, not in the Marxist, materialistic, atheistic sense which pretends to free man from oppression but subjects him to even greater tyranny, depriving him of all rights, personal and social, even that of worshipping God and of bringing God to all men!

The Exercises of St. Ignatius, though they are primarily concerned with *liberating* the person from the consequences of sin, do have within them concern for true social justice. The individual as a person has social responsibilities and his salvation depends on his proper carrying out of these responsibilities in accord with God's will. So, since the Exercises are directed to your salvation they must revolve in the orbit of social justice.

Pray for true social justice!

> *I ask to grow in faith, Lord, so that my actions may praise you and affect in some good way the lives of my brothers and sisters.*

In the light of the Social Encyclicals of the Church, reflect:

> *Remember your leaders who spoke the word of God to you; consider how their lives ended and imitate their faith* (Heb 13:7-8).

Even in early times the Spiritual Exercises affected those returning from making them in their homes, whether nobles, merchants, soldiers etc. During the retreat they reviewed in the light of the principle of "Love thy neighbor" their past conduct and resolved to treat others as brothers in Christ. Father General Arrupe says: "On many occasions, in the course of history, the Exercises have brought about conversions in the moral and individual order which have been concretized later on in radical changes of life and in generosity toward those in need."

Due to tremendous changes in the world which we are experiencing today there must be greater emphasis on the consideration during the Exercises of social responsiblity. The individual is a person, that is, one who has rights but these rights are to be exercised in the context of society, that is, in relation to the rights of others. So a specific effort must be made through the Exercises to transform attitudes and awaken consciences. There must be created a mentality of social justice.

The Spiritual Exercises you make, with this in mind, will enable you to see what is your proper function as an individual to the whole. Each right has a corresponding obligation and rights of individuals are to be exercised with consideration for the rights of others.

The Exercises will help you cultivate this attitude by emphasizing the following points: the evils brought about by *"cupido auri,"* inordinate attachments, improper use of goods, abuse of values; the need to fight against all disorder, cupidity, uncontrolled passions, all of which enslave man. You will be inculcated with Christ's attitude as Liberator and your duty to identify with him, to be a member of the true fraternity, Brotherhood in Christ. This battle against selfishness is to be waged until you, the retreatant, abandon self-love, self-will and self-interest.

Pray:

> *Father, you have given all peoples one common origin, and your will is to gather them as one family to yourself. Fill the hearts of all men with the fire of your love and the desire to ensure justice for all their brothers and sisters. By sharing the good things you give us may we secure justice and equality for every human being; an end to all divisions and a human society built on love and peace. "Take to heart the words which I enjoin on you today. Speak of them at home and abroad whether you are busy or at rest"* (Dt 6:5-7).

The Spiritual Exercises aim at a *continuous* conversion. This is not the time to be unconcerned, shrug your shoulders and say: "What can I do? I'll mind my own business. Who cares?" Never be anxious, but ever concerned! For St. Ignatius, as a basis for the whole process of continual reconversion, facing up to present problems of society, demands an ever-readiness, a going out of self. He wants you to offer yourself to God as a collaborator for liberating your neighbor from enslavement resulting from sin; injustice, hunger, poverty, oppression. A Man for All Seasons!

All of us are equally dependent on God. No one can be the slave of others. The right use of creatures demands that each one use them freely for pursuing his own complete happiness. There is demanded the re-creation of the new man renewed by the interior gift of the Spirit who brings about true social justice.

St. Ignatius says: "Therefore, we must make ourselves indifferent to all created things, as far as we are allowed free choice and are not under any prohibition" (Ex. 23). This "indifference" is the condition for social justice in every order: spiritual, material, personal, social.

This problem of social justice is something you should meditate on especially in the area of the First Week, in the meditations on sin, and in the meditation on the Kingdom in answer to the call of Christ. This you are to do in order to give greater proof of your love and to distinguish yourself in the service of the eternal King and Lord of all. You will not only offer yourself entirely for the work, but will act against your sensuality and carnal and worldly love, and make offerings of greater value and more importance.

Whatever you determine to do to bring about social justice is to be done in solidarity with Christ and with his Mystical Body, the Church. You are to make the commitment joined with the elimination of the roots of oppression and a search for the right means available for achieving it. So, I shall bring to your attention one of the present day means for answering Christ's call to social justice. It is the Communitarian Exercises of Father Lombardi, promulgated by the Better World Movement. I suggest that you read Father Lombardi's work published in an English translation by that Movement, entitled *The Communitarian Dimensions of Ignatius.*

The Communitarian Exercises

I wrote to Father Lombardi when I learned from his work *I esercizii communitarii* that some of his adherents rejected calling them Ignatian Exercises and held that he was the originator of a new form of Exercises, and that he himself was so humble that he thought them something derived from Ignatian Exercises. I told him that his Exercises were thoroughly Ignatian. They are based essentially on St. Ignatius' Exercises. Here, however, I shall speak to you about the social ministry as it is presented during a communitarian retreat.

Here there is a field of specific action in the Christian community and through it, towards other fields which in modern times have assumed great importance. Consideration is made on a family scale, on a wider and wider scale: workers, industrialists, nations, the world!

The communitarian exercises conclude with the consideration you are to make of your part in the most universal type of community, the entire People of God, and the whole race of man. The growing interdependence of the world renders most pressing the teaching about the unity of the human family.

You are a member of the new People of God, members of the Mystical Body of Christ, the Church, to which all men are invited. You are a part of that living and working community which, as a universal sacrament of salvation, endeavors to create unity among all men and unity between men and God. This task is not confined to pastors but belongs to you, too. You must collaborate with others and with the whole organism according to your individual talents so that both the whole and the parts may grow, reaching out to the fulness of unity.

Here, pause and pray!

> *Lord, hear my prayer! Grant that what has been promised by the sanctification wrought by your Word may be fulfilled everywhere with evangelical power and obtain the fulness of adoption which was foretold by the testimony of truth. "Pray that the word of the Lord may make progress and be hailed by many others even as it has been hailed by you"* (2 Th 2:1).

You are also a citizen of the world. The chains that bind you to all human beings indiscriminately are much stronger than those minor ones which bind you exteriorly to your fellow citizens. Consequently, every form of discrimination, social or cultural, for reasons of race, sex, age, color, language or religion, is to be rejected as contrary to the universal plan of God and the Spirit of Christ. Should you make communitarian exercises, you may well receive the grace after your retreat to be granted a profound ecclesial conscience along with a sense of universal brotherhood.

As a citizen, layman, priest or religious, you have the obligation to create actually the earthly city. Individually and collectively, you are to set the example in this area by being the first to practice the social doctrine you wish to arouse in others. Otherwise you will give a handle to those who taunt that, as Marx said "Religion is the opium of the people." He also said that Christian doctrine is good and beautiful but that Christians are the first not to live it out!

The Role of the Director

I made a distinction between what I call a *direct* retreat and a *directed* retreat. All retreats, no matter their form are "directed" in some way or other. There is always need of a guide whether for a group or for an individual. So now I shall tell you what you are to expect from the "director" or as St. Ignatius used to say "the one giving the retreat."

According to St. Ignatius the "one giving the retreat," but let us say, the director, must keep in mind for properly adapting the retreat to the following points which are taken from the Alphabetical Index of the *Spiritual Exercises*.

Visualize the director as a guide, while the real Director is the Holy Spirit.

Pray:

> *Almighty and eternal God, may the Holy Spirit come to dwell in me and make me a temple worthy of his glory. "Your words, Lord, are spirit and life"* (Jn 6:63).

Since the director is a guide, when he gives you the retreat he must ever keep in mind St. Ignatius' adaptability. The Exercises are essentially *your* encounter with God, so you must make them personally, and so any assistance you receive must be given according to your personal needs. No two persons are absolutely alike, so your director will listen to your needs. How many hours should you devote to prayer? At what times should you pray? On precisely what subjects should you make your meditations? How much and what kind of penance should you perform? Do you need instruction on prayer, examination of conscience, confession etc.?

The most important task of the director is to help you discern spirits, that is, whether the good Spirit, for instance your Guardian angel, or the evil spirit is inspiring you. Later on I shall go more into detail about this matter of discernment of spirits as found in the Spiritual Exercises (Nos. 313-336). The director, following these rules is to guide you and advise you as to the source of the movements of your soul, their meaning and the response you should make.

According to St. Ignatius, the director must keep in mind for properly adapting the Exercises to you the following points.

First, there is a practice (I do not say *the* practice) of the Exercises assumed for a concrete case of someone making a thirty day retreat for the first time and alone, not having previously made a choice, an election, of a state of life.

Second, he proposes a method for applying the Exercises under different circumstances. He also points out the purpose of each Week and of each meditation, the main steps of procedure, etc. He still, however, leaves the director to be the guide and arbiter of how everything is to be applied in view of his knowledge of what *you,* the retreatant have told him and so of what *you* need.

Third, he presents him with a theology, assuming many theological facts, for instance, man's creation, original sin, personal sin, Hell, Christ's Incarnation, Redemption, Resurrection, the coming of the Holy Spirit, Mary, Virgin Mother of God and our Mother, the Church, the Mystical Body of Christ, sanctifying grace, etc.

However, he expects the director, under the inspiration of the Holy Spirit, to know the theological applications of every fact, the exegetical explanation of the divine Word, in order to provide you, the retreatant, with Ignatian food properly prepared.

Fourth, there is finally the offering of his own spiritual experience of the Exercises, the itinerary of his own journey to God. Only the director, who knows by his own experience the inner and vital meaning imbedded therein, can impart to you not mere formulas but the very essence, the interior dynamism of the Spiritual Exercises.

So, in response to your director, pray:

> *God our Father, help me to hear your Son. Enlighten me with your word, that I may find the way to your glory. "My soul pines for your salvation. I hope in your word"* (Ps 119:81).

I shall conclude with a short statement on what should be your attitude toward your director. He is the great helper St. Ignatius wants you to use during your retreat. Though the Holy Spirit is the primary Director, working through the director and in you, it must never be forgotten that God works through secondary causes, in this case your retreat director.

During your retreat, though you must *listen* to the Holy Spirit, you must be sure it is the Holy and not the evil one to whom you are listening! Be careful for a busy mind can be the devil's workshop just as is an idle mind. Beware too of seeking novelties, being spiritually "curious," deceived by certain dangerous "spiritual" trends.

The better to avoid this you must be humble and sensible enough to ask the advice of your director. You must listen to him, so be frank and let him know all about your spiritual life so he can guide you. This knowledge will help him determine the content of your meditations, what religious practices you should adopt, what resolutions you should make etc. He will help you do what you have *personally* judged is right but at the same time enable you to distinguish whether you have been inspired by the Spirit of Truth or the Father of Lies.

Pray:

> *God our Father, you have sent us your Word to enlighten*

the world. Let your light shine upon me that I may recognize your greatness in your works and glorify you forever. "Speak, Lord, for your servant is listening. You have the words of eternal life" (Jn 6:68).

A Briefing on Your Tour From Time To Eternity

Before going into detail about the retreat you make, I would like to let you know that over the years I have given retreats, my main consideration was to follow not so much the letter of the Ignatian text as its spirit, that is, the spiritual "psychology" of the Spiritual Exercises. I gave retreats, for instance, closed ones to a group of really and truly social apostles—laymen and laywomen, black and white, a real "mixed" retreat!, five years in a row. Before giving the fifth retreat, the laywoman in charge told me that some of the members of the organization wanted a Lacouturian while others wanted an Ignatian retreat. After talking things over with me, she decided, as she said, she would have me continue giving them a non-Ignatian retreat. This despite the fact that each year I had given them the Spiritual Exercises of St. Ignatius following the psychological pattern of the Four Weeks but avoiding the repetition of the terms and expressions they had heard over and over again in other retreats. So, I shall now tell you what that psychological pattern is, a pattern which is to be adapted to you, the retreatant.

Here is what St. Ignatius has to say. "Four Weeks are assigned to the Exercises. The first part, is devoted to the consideration and contemplation of sin (The Purgative Way); the second part, is taken up with the life of Christ our Lord and Model up to Palm Sunday inclusive; the third part, treats of the Passion of Christ our Lord and Savior (the Illuminative way); the fourth part, deals with the Resurrection and ascension (the Unitive way)—Repentance, Enlightenment, Love. Awareness of the evil of sin; understanding of God's generosity and love; and, since love is sharing, union with God in love."

Pray:

God, our Father, your Word Jesus Christ spoke peace to a

*sinful world and brought mankind the gift of reconciliation
by the suffering and death he endured. Teach us, the people
who bear his name, to follow the example he gave us; may
our faith, hope and charity turn hatred to love, conflict to
peace, death to eternal life. "Happy are those who hear the
word in a spirit of openness; they shall bear fruit through
perseverance"* (Lk 8:15).

As I told you before, when you, during your retreat, under the
inspiration of the Holy Spirit, penetrate into the innermost rhythm of
the history of salvation, you will discover a pattern which is
constantly repeated in its essential characteristics. It is a pattern
which is found in the Old Testament in the way God guides the
Hebrew People, and in the New Testament in the way Jesus Christ
and the apostles proclaim the Good News of the Kingdom of God.

This pattern is also found in Vatican II in the way it attests to the
divine design in man and the world. It is this pattern that the Spiritual
Exercises follow in the spiritual itinerary you are to make in your
passage to God and in his passage to you. It is the practical
application of the history of salvation to you as an individual, an
"active" retreatant.

Under the inspiration of the Holy Spirit and the guidance of
your director, you will be given a strong experience of God. As I said
before, you must listen! Listen to God's word with open mind.
Though you are making the retreat as an individual you must ever
keep in mind that you are a person, a member of the Mystical Body
and everything you do or resolve to do must be made in a social,
communitarian context. You are part of a whole, the whole design
and mission of every Christian and of every man.

I stressed and I will stress again and again, that one of the
purposes of your retreat will be to *imitate,* to become like Christ in all
you do. So to arrive at such a radical conversion and so total a self-
surrender to Christ, through prayer, meditation and contemplation,
you must have an exact view of Christ in the Gospel. Finally, you will
reach a term, a greater realization of the presence of God, a presence
inspiring love, love being the sharing of your whole being with God
who will never be outdone in generosity.

Pray:

> *God, you created the whole world to show your power and overflowing love. Send forth your grace in my heart and renew the face of the earth by your Word.*

Reflect:

> *"Beloved, let us love one another because love is of God; everyone who loves is begotten of God and has knowledge of God. The man without love has known nothing of God, for God is love. God's love was revealed in our midst in this way: he sent his only Son to the world that we might have life through him, Love, then, consists in this: not that we have loved God, but that he has loved us and has sent his Son as an offering for our sins. Beloved, if God has loved us so, we must have the same love for one another"* (1 Jn 7-12).

So I speak to you *directly*. I urge you to make this Ignatian retreat. St. Ignatius tells you how. "It will be very profitable for one who is to go through the Exercises to enter upon them with magnanimity and generosity toward his Creator and Lord, and to offer him his entire will and liberty, that his Divine Majesty may dispose of him and all he possesses according to his most holy will." To insure this remember your purpose in making your retreat: "The conquest of self and the regulation of your life in such a way that no decision is made under the influence of any inordinate attachment" (Ex. 21).

At the close of your retreat St. Ignatius tells you to recite this prayer. I suggest you pray it now!

> *"Take, Lord, and receive all my liberty, my memory, my intellect, my will. All that I have and possess. Thou gavest it to me, to thee I return it. All is thine! Dispose of it according to thy will. Give me thy love and thy grace, for this is enough for me!"*

Reflect:

> *"Receive this message not as the words of man, but as truly the word of God"* (1 Th 2:13).

Chapter 2

A TOUR FROM TIME TO ETERNITY

We shall begin this chapter with a prayer!

> *Lord, may everything I do begin with your inspiration,*
> *continue with your help, and reach perfection under your*
> *guidance, through your word and your Spirit.*

St. Ignatius on defining the term "spiritual exercises" compares them
to bodily exercises: "For just as taking a walk, journeying on foot,
and running are bodily exercises, so we call spiritual exercises every
way of preparing and disposing the soul" (Ex. 1).

You will note that he says "every way," that is, the means to
attain the end of the Spiritual Exercises you will make, I hope, are
quite diverse depending, as I said, on "circumstances of time, place
and person." Even in St. Ignatius' own times, the Exercises were given
to fit the retreatant.

I am sure had Mary Magdalene come to make a retreat before
knowing Jesus, St. Ignatius would have given her quite a different
one than that he would have given to Elizabeth. So, no matter what
means you use, the important "sine qua non" is that they be suited for
attaining what *you* have in mind when you decide to make a retreat.

I, however, have chosen as title to this chapter not bodily
exercises but a *tour* to characterize the Exercises. I shall brief you on
this trip you may decide to make and tell you how and where you are
going. This is like the briefing you get from a tourist agency. If, before
going on your trip you learn from others about the advantages and

disadvantages you may meet, you will be prepared to enjoy the advantages and avoid the disadvantages. In travelling you have undoubtedly heard from others about the problems, the inconveniences even the dangers encountered enroute to the destination you have chosen. Or you have been told what is the best way to travel, the best things to do and to see, the best places to visit. What I tell you, I hope will serve to prepare you for enjoying your "tour", while the Spiritual Exercises *themselves* as well as your director will help you find out about, reflect on and apply it for reaching your ultimate destination—the salvation of your soul and the greater glory of God, the Ignatian *magis: ad majorem Dei gloriam!*

Pray:

> *Father of love, hear my prayers. Help me to know your will and to do it with courage and faith. "Everything God created is good; nothing is to be rejected when it is received with thanksgiving, for it is made holy by God's word and by prayer"* (1 Tm 4:5).

St. Ignatius will not only let you know where you are going on your tour, but will also let you know how to get there!

Prayer: Your Flight on the Wings of Prayer

I mentioned before that St. Ignatius was constantly aware of God's presence. This was a grace he received from God who made himself present to him through prayer. *Prayer is lifting up the mind to God, filling it with God.*

So, while you are on retreat you will be attending school, that is, the Spiritual Exercises are a school of prayer, one great prayer.

First Lesson: Examination of Conscience

The examination of conscience is a form of prayer and may be compared with the Holy Sacrifice of the Mass. We must realize that the word "sacrifice" has a meaning very appropriate for what is the essence of the Mass. It means "to make sacred." What is made sacred? Sacrifice occurs by the words of consecration, the gift we offer God, the Body, Blood, Soul and Divinity of Jesus Christ in his glorified Body still bearing the marks of his infinite love, the scars of the wounds on his hands feet and in his side. This gift is a supreme prayer of adoration, thanksgiving, reparation and petition.

When you make your examination of conscience you also offer up to God a prayer of adoration, putting yourself in the presence of God in praise, reverence and service; of thanksgiving, expressing your gratitude for the gifts he has given you; of reparation, expressing your sorrow for having offended him by your sins, faults and negligence; of petition, begging his grace to know your weaknesses and asking for that new life, light and love so you may know him more clearly, love him more dearly and follow him more nearly.

Pray:

> *Father I have wounded the heart of Jesus your Son, but he brings forgiveness and grace. Help me to prove my grateful love and make amends for my sins. "The Word is near you, on your lips and in your hearts, that is the word of faith we preach"* (Rm 10:8).

This practice of the examination of conscience is thoroughly explained in the *Spiritual Exercises.* As I said there is the particular examination of conscience (Ex. 24-26) and some counsels are given you to help to a more ready removal of the particular sin or fault being examined. Then there is the general examination (Ex. 32-41), the purpose of which is to purify the soul and aid you to improve your confessions.

There is a famous saying: Know thyself. This is the object of this examination of conscience, with the ulterior purpose of knowing how by self-improvement, that is, conversion, renewal, you will come to know whether you are doing God's will. As you will see in the *Principle and Foundation*, God's purpose in creating you is to praise, reverence and serve him and by this means to save your soul.

Pray:

> *God, you are the source of eternal light. I seek you from the*

*dawn of day. Enlighten me, that I may glorify you in word
and work and that my whole life may sing your praises. The
Gentiles were delighted when they heard this and responded
to the word of God with praise* (Ac 13:46).

Second Lesson; Meditation: Three Powers

The explanation of prayer which employs the three powers of the
soul: memory, intellect and will, is found in the very first exercise of
the First Week. It is one of the methods St. Ignatius proposes for you
to use during your retreat.

You will make a *preparatory prayer* in the presence of God. "All
your intentions, actions and operations may be directed purely to the
praise and service of his Divine Majesty" (Ex. 46). Then, the
composition of place: this may be a material place: a mountain where
Christ preached, or an imaginary place, your soul as a prisoner in
your corruptible body cast out to live among brute beasts (Ex. 47); a
prayer of petition: "You will ask God our Lord for what you want and
desire," (Ex. 48); you will then use your memory, intellect, and will;
and finally, you will make a *colloquy,* realizing God's presence and
making yourself present to him you ask for the grace which
corresponds to your spiritual situation."

In the Exercises there is *repetition.* Repetition is not only the
soul of scholarship but also of the spiritual life. This is not something
mechanical but that which enables you to "savor" the truths on which
you meditate. St. Ignatius advises you: "to pay attention to and dwell
on those points in which you have experienced greater consolation or
desolation or greater spiritual appreciation" (Ex. 62). This is to be
done in keeping with this further advice: "For it is not much
knowledge that fills and satisfies the soul but the intimate
understanding and relish (savor) of the truth" (Ex. 2).

Then there is the explanation of the use of the three powers:
memory, intellect and will.

St. Ignatius tells you how to use your memory in prayer. "This
will consist in using the memory to recall the sin of the angels, then
apply the understanding by reasoning upon this sin, then the will by
seeking to remember and understand all to be the more filled with

shame and confusion when I compare the one sin of the angels with the many sins I have committed . . . after using the memory to recall the details of this first sin, then use the understanding to think over the matter more in detail, and then the will to rouse more deeply the emotions (Ex 50).

Such a use of the *memory* involves the choice of a definite object on which you are going to meditate, an objective fact in the history of salvation. It is a concentration, a control over the memory's tendency to wander, an opening of your mind to the Mystery of God, as found in the Gospel or in the Revelation of Christ. It also helps you to "savor" and preserve this memory in your heart, as a token of God's love, presenting you with a challenge to return love for love.

St. Ignatius tells you to ask our Blessed Mother for: "A deep knowledge of your sins; an understanding of the disorder of your actions; a knowledge of the world" (Ex. 62).

In imitation of Mary *ponder,* use your intellect, reflect on what you are meditating and you will come more and more to realize what these truths mean to you personally as a member of the Mystical Body of Christ in the plan of salvation.

St. Ignatius tells you how to use your *will* in prayer: "Beg of God our Lord that all your intentions, actions and operations be directed purely to the praise and service of his Divine Majesty" (Ex.46). Later he instructs you; "the will is to rouse more deeply the emotions." This last excerpt shows that the will is not only the faculty for deciding, resolving, but is also the faculty of love and affection; love is sharing. You can exercise it in desires, regrets, requests, in the will to imitate Christ and, in many instances, you will exercise it in colloquies in which there is, as a movement of grace, an aspiration to love God under the inspiration of the Holy Spirit.

Before I explain the colloquy, talking to God, talk to him now.

> *God our Father, no secret is hidden from you, for every heart is open to you and every wish is known. Fill my heart with the light of your Holy Spirit to free my thoughts from sin that I may perfectly love you and fittingly praise you.*

Finally, there is the colloquy. St. Ignatius says: "The colloquy is made by speaking exactly as one friend speaks to another, or as a servant speaks to a master, now asking him for a favor, now blaming himself for some misdeed, now making known his affairs to him, and seeking advice in them" (Ex.54).

But the first colloquy is so beautiful I must present it: "Imagine Christ our Lord present before you upon the cross. Speak to him: "Jesus, how is it that though you are the Creator, you have stooped to become man, and to pass from eternal life to death here in time, that thus you might die for my sins?"

Then reflect and say: "Jesus, what have I done for you? What am I doing for you? What ought I do for you?" You alone know what answers you should give.

Third Lesson: Application of the Senses

When you meditate during your retreat St. Ignatius tells you to apply your five senses by your imagination. You will imagine details: persons, places, sounds, etc. of the subject on which you are meditating. It will be a wonderful experience if you have not cultivated a creative imagination, especially in these days of passive imagination when radio, television, etc. supply such objects.

The first specific instance in the *Spiritual Exercises* is the meditation on hell: *sight:* see the vast fires, and the souls enclosed in bodies of fire; *hearing:* hear the wailing, the howling, the cries and blasphemies against Christ; *smell:* note the odor of the smoke, the sulphur, the filth and corruption; *taste:* experience the bitterness of tears, sadness and remorse of conscience; *touch:* feel the flames.

In view of the feeling you must have, pray!

> *Holy Michael, the Archangel, defend me in battle, be my protection against the malice and snares of the devil. Restrain him, O God, I humbly beseech thee and do thou, Prince of the heavenly hosts, by divine power cast into hell Satan and the other evil spirits who roam about the earth seeking the destruction of souls. From every evil way I withhold my feet that I may keep your words* (Ps 101, 102, 119).

Election: the Motor Power of Your Tour

By this analogy I want to impress you with the importance of your making the right choice (election). This motive power will enable you to reach your destination; *the love of God, and you will learn that God is love.* It may be said that in the *Principle and Foundation* you obtain knowledge of God, a knowledge which, during your retreat, grows deeper and deeper, especially in the contemplations of the Second and Third Weeks. Thus inspired, your emotions are aroused and your will motivated so that what you have *chosen* becomes permeated and animated by that love which St. Ignatius defines as sharing, sharing in all that you are and have. This is beautifully expressed in the prayer I gave you before and which you are to repeat now: *Take, Lord, and receive. . . "*

One of the greatest gifts God has given you is your free will. But it is also a very risky gift: By it you can accept God and his design for your salvation, his love. But you can also say with Satan: "I will not serve," rejecting God's love. "He came unto his own and his own received him not!" So you have a choice and that is why St. Ignatius emphasizes the importance of this in his Spiritual Exercises. And this is also why your director will help you make the right choice.

You will also recall that, though God walked in the Garden with Adam and Eve, they were deceived by the evil spirit. So you will understand why St. Ignatius will teach you how to discern which spirit, the Holy Spirit or the evil spirit, is the one leading you to make a choice. This is known as *Discernment of Spirits* (Ex. 313-328).

However, in the election you are to make, the choice is concerned with one between good things. I might call it Christian free will which is used when you want to do what God wills, that is, "reverence, praise and serve him." In your retreat you are seeking to find the will of God in the disposition of your life and the salvation of your soul. So the decision you are to make will bring about a union of wills, the divine will and your will, the will of a creature who is disposed to accept that divine will. I think that no one can improve on St. Ignatius' "common sense" explanation of what he calls "making a choice of a way of life" (Ex.169-184). Here is what he says:

In every good choice, as far as depends on you, your

intention must be simple. You must consider only the end for which you are created, that is, for the praise of God our Lord and for the salvation of your soul. Hence, whatever you choose must help you to this end for which you are created.

You must not subject and fit the end to the means, but the means to the end. . . . Therefore your first aim should be to seek to serve God, which is the end, and only after that, if it is more profitable to have a benefice or marry, for these are means to the end. (Of course, in place of these alternatives, there are others which your director will help you choose). Nothing must move you to use such means, or to deprive yourself of them, save only the service and praise of God our Lord and the salvation of your soul" (Ex. 119).

As to the alternatives I mentioned in the parenthesis above, St. Ignatius says: "It is necessary that all matters about which you wish to make a choice be either indifferent or good in themselves, and *such that they are lawful within our holy Mother, the hierarchical Church,* and not bad or opposed to her" (Ex. 170). The choice may be made among three different objects the state of life, revocable choices, reform of life or renewal. Of course, your director will advise you on the area in which your election is to be made, one primarily in accord with why you are making the retreat.

That is why, during your retreat, you must be open and frank with him so that you get the most out of your retreat. No matter in which state, married, single, religious, priest, brother or nun, the concept of divine vocation, call assumes that God disposes of everything in your life. God does this within the design of salvation realized in Christ, in his Mystical Body, particularly in the Church.

I think you may be more interested in reformation and in renewal. "Reformation of your way of living in the state you are now in" (Ex. 189). So, "It will be profitable for you, in place of a choice, to propose a way for you to reform your manner of living in your state by setting before yourself the purpose of your creation and your life and position, namely, the glory of God our Lord and the salvation of your soul. You are to desire nothing except the greater glory of God our Lord as the aim of all you do. For you must keep in mind that in all that concerns the spiritual life your progress will be in proportion to your surrender of self-love and of your own will and interest" (Ex. 189)

Pray:

> *God our Father, teach me to find new life through penance, keep me from sin and help me love through our Lord Jesus Christ your Son. Let my cry come before you, O Lord; in keeping with your word, give me discernment* (Pss 109, 119).

The choice made by your human will is to be an encounter with God's will. You will gradually learn what his will is. To help you in this, with the assistance of your director and, of course, the Holy Spirit, St. Ignatius gives you some norms for determining at what "time" your decision will meet with God's will.

Although God may give you for making your choice a grace such as St. Ignatius was given on his retreat at Manresa, and though you may have undergone the trial of the deceits of the evil spirit, as did Jesus himself when tempted by Satan, most likely you will make your choices, whether they be greater or lesser, in an aura of tranquillity. You will do so when your soul is not agitated by different spirits, and has free and peaceful use of its natural powers. So St. Ignatius will tell you how to come to a decision.

Of course, he would suggest you address yourself to God in prayer!

> *Father of light, in you is found no shadow of change but only fulness of light and limitless truth. Open my heart to the voice of your Word and free me from the original darkness which shadows vision. Restore my sight that I may look upon your Son who calls me to repentance and a change of heart. "Get wisdom, get understanding! Do not forget or turn aside from the words I utter* (Pr 4:5).

Think over what you want to choose. You must have *balance*. St. Ignatius uses the term indifference. That is, you must strive to be without any inordinate attachment pro or con. You must beg God to move your will as to what you should do to promote his glory in regard to the matter in question. Weigh the advantages and disadvantages. St. Ignatius would write down on a sheet of paper the pros and the cons and then make a judgment, based on what is more reasonable rather than on feeling. A real Master of common sense! Finally, you are to turn to prayer and in the presence of God offer him your choice that he may deign to accept it if it is for his greater service and praise (Ex. 178-183).

Should you find that your sensual inclinations are strong then St. Ignatius proposes you call on the motive of love so that you choose solely out of love of God in response to his love. To guarantee this, ask yourself what you will advise, not a friend or a relative, but a complete stranger to do under such circumstances, in order to attain perfection. Also, ask yourself, were you on your deathbed, what would you then decide (Ex.184-187). So, you see how practical St. Ignatius was and why I have always regarded him as a great administrator, "a Man for All Seasons!"

In conclusion, you can clearly see how the Exercises will affect your life after your retreat and how helpful they will be for bringing you closer to God, faithful to the resolutions you were inspired to make by the Holy Spirit.

Discernment of Spirits: Direction Finder

> *Father, you give us food from heaven. By my sharing in this mystery, teach me to judge wisely the things of earth and to love the things of heaven. "Man does not live by bread alone, but on every word that comes from the mouth of God"* (Mt 4:4).

On a tour at times the plane takes a wrong course due to failure of its instruments to receive proper directions from the "tower" or due, rarely we hope, to misunderstanding by the pilot of the directions given, and even more rarely we hope, due to the plane being taken over by a kidnapper who intends to hold the plane and its contents hostage! With the help of your director and the Holy Spirit you will find out through Discernment of spirits (Ex. 313-327) whether you are on the right course.

Pray:

> *As your people, we lift our voices to you, Father. We know the evil of our ways. So we pray to be faithful through the light of your Spirit and happy under your protecting hand.*

There are two sets of rules given by St. Ignatius for the First Week— the Purgative way—and for the Second Week—Illuminative Way. They are "rules for understanding to some extent the different movements produced in the soul and for recognizing those that are good to admit them, and those that are bad, to reject them."

As I said the defect in your range finder may be intended by someone who wants to hold you hostage. He pretends to be a friend, the Holy Spirit, but is really an enemy, Satan! To help you keep on your course, is your director's essential task. He will help you distinguish between information and misinformation, by the use of the best written guide book, St. Ignatius' *Spiritual Exercises.*

Instead of quoting from the text, I shall take excerpts which bring out the essentials.

The Type of Passengers on Board

St. Ignatius mentions three types: those who go from one mortal sin to another; those who go on earnestly striving to cleanse their souls from sin and seek to rise in the service of God to greater perfection; those souls which are progressing to greater perfection.

Tactics of the Good Spirit and of the Evil Spirit

The way the Father of Lies employs is diverse from that employed by the Good Spirit, and this is true for both the First Week and the Second Week.

Tactics of the First Week. In the case of one going from one mortal sin to another, the *enemy* proposes apparent pleasures; the *Good Spirit* arouses the sting of conscience and remorse. In the case of one striving to cleanse the soul from sin and seeking to rise to greater perfection, the method is the reverse.

Tactics of the Second Week. God and his angels, give true happiness and spiritual joy; the evil one fights against this by proposing fallacious reasonings and deceptions. Both the good Spirit and the bad spirit may give consolation; the *good Spirit* for the progress of the soul to perfection; the *evil spirit* to draw the soul to his own perverse intentions.

Advice of the Pilot

Just as the weather changes on a flight, so too the climate of your soul is subject to changes. St. Ignatius tells you about them.

Spiritual Consolation: it is an interior movement of the soul of love of God above all creatures; tears well up that move to love of God due to sorrow for sins, the sufferings of Christ etc.; every increase of faith, hope and love, every interior joy invite us to what is heavenly and to the salvation of one's soul filling it with peace and quiet in Christ our Lord (Ex. 316).

Spiritual desolation: it is the opposite. There is darkness, turbulence, inclination to the low and earthly, want of faith, hope and love (Ex. 317).

Now, when you are travelling by plane and the weather changes, a strong wind blows up or it rains etc. you follow the pilot's advice. So too, follow the advice that your director, inspired by the Holy Spirit and St. Ignatius will give you. I urge you to read over prayerfully and carefully what St. Ignatius says in Ex. 313-336.

In time of desolation never make any change in what you have resolved or decided on before. However, do increase prayer and meditation etc. Keep in mind that, even though you have that dangerous gift of free will, God is still with you. This desolation may be due to your tepidity and sloth; God may be trying you; God wishes to give you true knowledge of yourself and a realization that spiritual gifts and grace come from him.

St. Ignatius tells you how you are to react against the wiles of the devil. Face up to the enemy! The enemy is a weakling before a show of strength; a tyrant if he gets his way; also he looks for your weak points before he attacks. The devil wants to remain hidden. So do not conceal things from your director so he can warn you about his deceitfulness. The devil poses as, what St. Ignatius calls, an angel of light.

Before I explain in the next chapter what your retreat will be essentially, the Four Way tour you are about to make.

Pray:

> *Pray God, help me to apply myself to the Spiritual Exercises. May I penetrate more deeply into the mystery of Christ and lead a life worthy of it. "Receive and submit to the word planted in you; it can save your souls"* (Mk 7:24-30).

Chapter 3

THE PRINCIPLE AND FOUNDATION—FIRST WEEK

Let us pray!

God our Father, open my eyes to see your hand at work in the splendor of creation, in the beauty of human life. Touched by your hand our world is holy. Help me to cherish the gifts that surround me to share your blessings with my brothers and sisters and to experience the joy of life in your presence. "Turn to me and be safe, all you ends of the earth, for I am God, there is no other! By myself I swear, uttering my just decree and my unalterable word" (Is 45:22-24).

I mentioned that St. Ignatius divided his Spiritual Exercises into four Weeks, three stages of your tour. The subject matter of this chapter will be a briefing given you before your tour, an introduction to your whole retreat and information on the four Weeks.

The Principle and Foundation

"Man is created to praise, reverence and serve God our Lord and by this means to save his soul; other creatures are created for man to help him to attain this end... hence, man is to use them insofar as they help rid himself of them, insofar as they hinder its attainment. Our one desire and choice should be what is more conducive to the end for which we are created" Ex. 23).

The Principle and Foundation is primarily an introduction to the Exercises as a whole. You, as a retreatant must regard it as a briefing as to where you are going, how you will get there and what you will do on the way. However, for a while, at least, I shall depart from my analogy of a tour. I shall show you how the Spiritual Exercises you make will help you answer some ordinary questions. When you see something you usually ask questions, "What is it for?" "How do I work it?" "How much is it?" "Where can I get it?" You continue, "What do I do?" "How do I do it?" "How can I do it?" "Who will help me?" There may be other questions too.

You are going to make your retreat to find the answers to such questions with the assistance of your director, but *primarily through your own efforts under the inspiration of the Holy Spirit.* As I said, you will use your memory, intellect and will, created as you are in the image and likeness of the Triune God. You will do so with a soul infused by God and as a recipient of the new life principle restored by the Word of God from the very moment of repentance of our First Parents for their sin of pride and disobedience. You will be helped by the Light of that Word and the Love of his Holy Spirit to have that Life restored so that you can reach your supernatural destination. Never forget you are children of God, sharing in wondrous ways his divinity.

So pray!

> *Father, Creator and Redeemer of mankind, you decreed and your word became man, born of the Virgin Mary. May I come to share the divinity of Christ, who humbled himself to share my human nature. "The word of God became man and lived among us. He enabled those who accepted him to become the children of God"* (Jn 1:14).

The Ultimate in Common Sense: Ignatian Indifference

St. Ignatius advises: "Therefore we must make ourselves indifferent to all created things." This is the ultimate in common sense. Unfortunately due to the consequences of original sin common sense is one of the rarest of all commodities: Means are to be used to attain ends. You do not drive a thumbtack with a sledge-hammer: You do not buy a pig in a poke: Before you buy a horse, look in its mouth: Look before you leap: If this or that tool is equally practical, use either one; When one is more efficient than the other, use it, for it is "that which is most conducive for the end for which it is made—for which you are created."

So, back to our "tour" and pray!

> *God, you manifest your truth as a beacon to light up the right road for those who have lost their way. Grant to all who profess the one faith to reject whatever is contrary to your name and seek the things that are in harmony with it. "From every evil way I withhold my feet that I may keep your words"* (Ps 101, 102, 119).

You will recall, and I suggest you re-read what I told you about these points: the *history of salvation, prayer, election and discernment of spirits.* You can see readily that these factors which pervade the whole Exercises, are found in germ in the Principle and Foundation. They will be developed throughout the retreat and you are well aware that, with the help of your director, you are to apply them to yourself.

Here is a prayer found in Father Puhl's *Spiritual Exercises of St. Ignatius:*

> *Soul of Christ, santify me, Body of Christ, save me, Blood of Christ, inebriate me, water from the side of Christ, wash me, Passion of Christ, strengthen me. O Good Jesus, hear me! Within thy wounds, hide me, permit me not to be separated from thee. From the wicked foe defend me. At the hour of my death call me and bid me come to thee that with thy saints I may praise thee for ever and ever. Amen.*

First Week of the Three Way Tour—Purgative Way

Let us begin with this prayer!

> *Jesus, you are our Savior, the author of inconceivable salvation. Hear the prayer of your faithful. Free us from the slavery of the devil and show us, your redeemed members,*

*the glory of the eternal Father. "Receive and submit to the
word planted in you; it can save your souls"* (Mk 7:24:30).

St. Ignatius has logically divided his Spiritual Exercises into four
Weeks: the first, the purgative way; the second and third weeks, the
illuminative way; the fourth week, the unitive way. May these be steps
on your "tour" to your spiritual destination. The *Principle and
Foundation* gave you a briefing; the final exercises, the *Contemplation to attain the love of God,* will bring you to your destination.

Now, before I tell you about these stages of your tour, I want to
bring out something most essential to your retreat: *the Christo-
centricity of the Spiritual Exercises.* Jesus Christ, the Second Person
of the Blessed Trinity, true God, the only begotten Son of the Father,
true man, conceived by the Holy Spirit and born of the Blessed Virgin
Mary, the God-Man, is the foundation of your hope that your part in
the history of salvation during your retreat and afterwards will bring
you to your final destiny in the heart of Christ, his Father and the
Holy Spirit. I want you to realize that salvation is not only history in
the sense of past events but a mystery of the Eternal Now. Even before
Jesus was born of Mary, you *are* present to God!

In order to bring out even more clearly this mystery of the
Eternal Now, I shall tell you about one of my professors some years
ago. He is now dead but I still remember him daily at Mass even
though he was a Jew and a professed Marxist atheist!.

One day in class he made some disparaging remarks ridiculing
the Church's doctrine on the indissolubility of marriage. I made it a
practice never to object to anything a professor said in class but
rather, in order to protect his reputation, I would go to his office and
make my complaint in private. I did so in this case.

The next day, the professor went to the blackboard. In the
presence of the students, hardly any of them Catholic, he drew at one
end a large ALPHA, at the other, an OMEGA. In between he drew a
large cross with the Body of Christ nailed to it, with streams of blood
flowing from his wounds. Then he told the amazed students what he
called the Church's concept of the world: All those living before the
birth of Jesus, upon dying were saved by the *anticipated* merits of
Christ; all those living after his birth, on dying were and will be saved

by his *applied* merits. So in this sense Christ is the Eternal Now and had you in mind in his design of salvation from the beginning to the end of time!

Keep this in mind during your whole retreat from the beginning to the end, and no matter how much you may have offended him by sin, rejecting thereby his Father's love, his love and the love of the Holy Spirit, he has ever had you in mind from Alpha to Omega.

Thereby, too, you will realize that in this first Week, under the purgative way, you will see from what man and you are cleansed: the rejection of God's love and the effects of that rejection, cleansed in the Blood and Water flowing from the wounds of Christ. My professor also said that, through this blood flowing from Christ's wounds the sacraments, one of which is matrimony, receive their efficacy!

Here is why St. Ignatius says: "the purgative way, which corresponds to the Exercises of the First Week" (Ex. 10) According to Genesis "The Lord God formed man out of clay" (2:7). But it was clean clay and it was not until it was muddied by man himself that it needed cleansing and purging. This mud is sin.

Pray:

> *God our Father, no secret is hidden from you, for every heart is open to you and every wish is known. Fill my heart with the light of your Holy Spirit to free my thoughts from sin so that I may perfectly love you and fittingly praise you. "You are clean already thanks to the word I have spoken to you"* (Jn 15:3).

The Meaning of Sin: Rejection of God

"Sin is a free and deliberate transgression of the law of God (responsibility); any deliberate turning away, however slight, from God, *our ultimate end,* to embrace some finite good in opposition to the law of God (egotism): The essential nature of sin is rebellion against God (pride) (New American Bible).

In the light of this definition recall St. Ignatius' definition of the Spiritual Exercises: "Every way of preparing and disposing the soul to rid itself of all inordinate attachments and, after their removal, of seeking and finding the will of God in the disposition of our life for the salvation of our soul" (Ex. 1).

Therefore, first you are to learn what sin is, what are its effects which will help you determine to cleanse yourself of this "mud" and then find out what are the measures God has given you to cleanse yourself: fear of punishment; (the fires of hell), *plus (not or)* contriteness for having rejected His infinite love as manifest in his Son's sacrifice on the Cross and the constant helpful presence of his Mystical Body in the Church and in you as a member.

> *Lord, you brought me to the fountain of life like a tree planted near running waters. Grant that I may bear perpetual fruit through the cross of your Son. "Strip away all that is filthy, every vicious excess. Humbly welcome the word that has taken root in you with the power to save you"* (Jn 1:21).

In his *Spiritual Exercises,* between the *Principle and Foundation* and the *Exercises on Sin and its Consequences* (Ex. 45-81), St. Ignatius instructs you on how to examine your conscience in preparation for making a general confession. After these Exercises of the First Week he treats of the penances you should perform with the advise of your director.

These are the meditations St. Ignatius proposes: the first is on the first three sins: of the angels, of Adam and Eve, (Original Sin), and a particular personal mortal sin; the second is on your own sins (repetition); then, meditation on hell. He suggests that, should the director judge proper, you will benefit by meditations on death, other punishments of sin, judgment, etc.

Sin and its Effects According to Vatican II

Here is what Christ's Mystical Body, the hierarchical Church holds—and so you are to hold—about sin. I quote this to show you that, though God is love, sin is still sin and the rejection of that love. If unrepented, sin deserves punishment, purgatory if venial, hell if mortal. This is what St. Ignatius held in his day.

The *The Pastoral Constitution on the Church Today* describes the modern rejection of God's love: "By virtue of the Gospel committed to her the Church proclaims the rights of man. She acknowledges and greatly esteems the dynamic movements of today by which these rights are everywhere fostered. Yet *these movements must be penetrated by the spirit of the Gospel and protected against any kind of false autonomy.* For we are tempted to think we are exempt from every requirement of divine law. But this does not enhance the maintenance of the dignity of the human person but its annihilation" (Ex. 41).

Despite some doubts expressed by some neo-theologians, the Council explicitly affirms the existence of that on which you will meditate: namely, original and actual sin.

"Although man was made by God in a state of holiness from the very dawn of history, man abused his liberty, at the urging of personified Evil. Man set himself against God and sought fulfillment—apart from God—and served the creature rather than the Creator.

"Examining his heart, man finds that he has inclinations toward evil . . . man is split within himself. As a result, all of human life, whether individual or collective, shows itself to be a dramatic struggle between good and evil, between light and darkness" (Ex. 13).

An Ignatian Concept of Sin: Interruption of Dialogue Between God and Man

Before I comment on St. Ignatius' concept of sin, I suggest the following prayers in tune with the Second Preludes of the Exercises of the First Week.

> *My Lord and God, make me feel shame and confusion, because I see how many have been lost on account of a single mortal sin, and how many times I have deserved eternal damnation, because of the many grievous sins that I have*

committed. My Lord and my God, grant me a growing and intense sorrow and tears for my sins. Grant me, too, a deep sense of the pain which the lost suffer, that if through my faults I forget your love, at least the fear of these punishments will keep me from falling into sin. "I call upon you for you will answer me, O God. Incline your ear to my words" (Ps 17).

There is a very important concept of sin which you are to ponder during your retreat. I have said that the Spiritual Exercises are a Word of God, that is a conversation between you and God. Sin is an interruption of this dialogue. This interruption is caused by pride and confusion.

You will recall that man, especially today, is led astray by pride and the resultant confusion—Ignatian signs of the Devil, and in imitation of his "I will not serve." So, man wants to do what he pleases, rejects any law of God, even the Ten Commandments and the precepts and teachings of the Church.

This pride leads to confusion. For, paradoxically, when there is brought about by sin a drastic limitation on his ability to choose and thereby exercise his own free will, he chains himself to the flesh and to the concupiscence arising from within and becomes a slave of Satan, and a rebel against his God, his Lord, his Savior Jesus Christ.

Pray:

Lord Jesus, gentle and humble of heart, you promised your kingdom to the humble and the childlike. Never permit pride to rule my heart, that I may accept your gentle yoke and obtain mercy and glory from your Father.

Lord, have compassion on your Church. She is still on her way to you. Look at her distress and hear her prayers. Rescue me from the confusion of our time and make me march steadfastly on the way to you. "Let him who has ears heed the Spirit's words to the Church" (Rm 3:6).

Acknowledgment of God's Justice, Hope in His Mercy

Now, in your meditations on sin, you are not to be discouraged. You must have faith, that is, belief in the truths on which you are meditating but at the same time have *hope,* a hope based on the realization, deeper and deeper, that you must have *love,* love of God, and love of yourself and of your neighbor out of love for God. Recall that when the disciples had reason to fear the storm on the lake, Christ rebuked them: "O you of little faith, why did you doubt?" Now here is a good time to make the Act of Faith.

Now that you have this consciousness of sin you come to the tremendous fact of *hope.* You have received a greater knowledge of sin and consequently realize how distant you may be from God— through venial or mortal sin. Just as the Israelites in Egypt realized how far they were from the Promised Land, now you too realize how far you may be. But, just as they came to know that Moses, inspired by God, would lead them out of Egypt, you too know and will ponder on the fact that there is hope for you. You will return to your Fatherland through the salvation wrought by his Son, Jesus Christ. Now make an Act of Hope.

Just as the Israelites before reaching the Promised Land had to undergo trials and tribulations, you too must realize that ahead of you is an eschatological goal. On your journey to the Fatherland you too will be exposed, during your retreat and after, to the risks of that journey. You will constantly be faced with decisions as to which turn on the road you should take. Just as the Israelites had their guides, so too you will have yours: the Holy Spirit, the Word of God, the Mystical Body, the Church, and, during your retreat, your director to help you follow the right road.

The Spiritual Exercises will be an Exodus en route to the Fatherland. Pray, then, to Christ and his blessed Mother, asking your Mother and your Brother, to obtain for you a greater awareness of the meaning of *love,* love of God and of your neighbor whom you must love as yourself for love of God. That you may not reject this love implore the Holy Spirit to give you a deeper knowledge of your sins and a feeling of abhorrence of them, an understanding of the disorder of your actions, so that filled with horror of them, you may amend your life, put it in order and also have knowledge of the world, so that filled with horror of whatever creatures may prevent you from reaching your destination, you will put them aside as worldly and vain. All this *ad majorem Dei gloriam!* Conclude with an Act of Love—charity.

The Loss of God: the Greatest Pain of Hell

St. Ignatius, while accepting the Church's doctrine on Hell, does not see in it anything counter to God's love. And neither did Dante. In his *Inferno*, Canto 111, 4-6 he tells of a sign over the gates of hell: "Justice moved by High Maker; Divine Power made me, Wisdom Supreme, and Primal Love."

St.Ignatius tells you that your primary motive for avoiding sin is God's love, but that God has provided you with another motor should the first fail to function: "fear of the consequences." Perhaps during this First week, you may deeply sense this "fear." He wants you to apply the methods of prayer known as that of the *Three Powers:* memory, intellect and will, and of the *Five Senses,* when you meditate on this subject.

In conclusion of this commentary on the Spiritual Exercises of the First Week, I shall remind you of the meaning of the colloquy I gave you before, that is, "speaking to God as one friend speaks to another." I also remind you of what you are to ask yourself: "What have I done for Christ? What am I doing for Christ? What shall I do for Christ?" In this way you will ready yourself for going on with your retreat wherein you will find the answers to these questions through the inspiration of the Holy Spirit.

> *God our Father, you loved the world so much, you gave your only Son to free us from the ancient power of sin and death. Help us who wait for his coming, and lead us to true liberty. Lord, our God, help us to prepare for the coming of Christ your Son. May he find us waiting, eager in joyful prayer.*

Chapter 4

THE KINGDOM—THE SECOND WEEK: IMITATION OF CHRIST

Pray:

> *Eternal Lord of all things, in the presence of thy infinite goodness, and of thy glorious mother, and of all the saints of thy heavenly court, this is the offering of myself which I make with thy favor and help. I protest that it is my earnest desire and my deliberate choice, provided only it is for thy greater service and praise, to imitate thee in bearing all wrongs and all abuse and all poverty, both actual and spiritual, should thy most holy majesty deign to choose and admit me to such a state and way of life.*

The above prayer, taken from the *Spiritual Exercises*, is intended to help you show greater generosity in response to the call of Christ our Lord. This call of Christ is not only to avoid offending his Father by sin (the aim of the First Week) but to inspire you through his Holy Spirit to choose that which is *magis*, that is, more conducive to bringing you to salvation in accordance with his Father's will, passing from the low plane of avoidance of sin to the very highest peak of love.

The Kingdom of Christ Eternal Lord of All Things

This meditation presents the call of an earthly king and the response of his subjects and its purpose is to make you realize with what greater loyalty you should respond to the call of Christ our Lord, the Eternal King. Some writers think that presenting Christ as a king to retreatants of today is quite irrelevant. If you feel this way, then think of Christ as your Friend with whom you share the joys, sorrows, pains and pleasures of daily life. You recall St. Ignatius said that in your colloquies in the First Week you could do this.

Pray:

> Lord, you saved me through your Son, our eternal King and High Priest. Grant that his pure offering may be brought from the rising of the sun even to its setting over the whole earth and that all nations will be led to him as one holy people. "Turn to me and be safe, all you ends of the earth, for I am God, there is no other! By myself I swear, uttering my just decree and my unalterable word" (Is 45:22-24).

Time and again I have said you must ponder during your retreat on how you can come to know Christ more clearly, that you love him more dearly and follow him more nearly. Then, after you have done this, do what St. Ignatius told you in the First Week: ask yourself: "What have I done for Christ? What am I doing for Christ? What should I do for Christ?" The Holy Spirit throughout the next Weeks will inspire your answer, and you will answer more generously the more you contemplate in your meditations on the life of Christ, especially in the Second and Third Weeks, what Christ has done for you!

Pray:

> I Lord, I am not worthy that thou shouldst come to me, but speak the words of comfort, my spirit healed shall be. And humbly I'll receive thee, the Bridegroom of my soul, no more by sin to grieve thee, nor fly thy sweet control. Mighty Eternal Spirit, unworthy though I be, prepare me to receive thee and trust the Word to me.

Father da Camara says that St. Ignatius' favorite spiritual reading was the *Following of Christ*, by Thomas Kempis. So it is not surprising that he advises you "during the Second Week and thereafter, that it will be very profitable to read some passages from *"The Following of Christ"* (Ex. 100). That is why though you may have a copy of this inspired work, I have quoted and will quote passages from it. *"Follow Christ and learn to condemn what is passing."* "No follower of mine shall ever walk in darkness" (Jn 8:12).

These are words from the mouth of Christ which encourage us to imitate his life, if we would be truly enlightened and healed from all blindness of heart. Therefore our main endeavor must be to penetrate deeply into the life of Jesus Christ.

"For the teachings of Christ without exception surpass everything the Saints have taught, and he who has Christ's Spirit, must find therein hidden manna.

"But it happens that many who often hear the Gospel nonetheless feel in their hearts little desire for it, because they do not have the Spirit of Christ.

"He who will fully understand and savor the teachings of Christ must earnestly strive to make of his own life a second life of Jesus" (*The Following of Christ* Bk I, Ch. 1).

Jesus is your model and in everything and in every way you must conform your life to his. That is the primary reason for you to make the Spiritual Exercises.

Pray:

> *Father, your Son became like me when he revealed himself in my nature. Help me to become more like him, who lives and reigns with you and the Holy Spirit, one God, for ever and ever. "The Son is the reflection of the Father's glory, the exact representation of the Father's being, and he sustains all things by his powerful word"* (Heb.1:3).

Christ is *Lord*. He is the one whom we are to serve; Christ is *Servant*. He came to do the will of his Father; Christ is our *example*. He came to show us how to do the will of his Father. So your generosity in answer to his call is to be measured by how closely you imitate Christ. This response is to be voluntary, of your free will. To dedicate yourself to Christ is not to be coerced. Attracted by his love, you wish to share with him and to do what you must to come to know him more perfectly. This you will try to do especially in the Second Week where you will learn not only who he is, but also what he wants you to do, that is, the will of his Father who sent him.

St. John, in the Prologue of his Gospel, tells you: "But to as many as received him he gave the power of becoming sons of God." So, Christ is not only your King and Friend, he is your Brother. On your retreat you will come to realize more and more what this means, not only for you personally but for your brothers and sisters in Christ. St. Ignatius reminds you of this:

"Consider how the Lord of all the world chooses so many persons, apostles, disciples etc., and sends them throughout the whole world to spread his sacred doctrine among all men, no matter what their state or condition" (Ex. 145). You, too, are to regard yourself as a "disciple" and so spread his sacred doctrine no matter in what state or condition you may be.

So pray!

> Lord, my help and guide, make your love the foundation of my life. May my love for you express itself in my eagerness to do good for others. I charge you to preach the word, to stay with this task whether convenient or inconvenient"...(2 Tm. 4:2).

Christ is a unique model. By imitating him you do not only become like him but you become other Christs. You share by adoption in the plenitude of his divinity: "Of his fulness we have all received." This fulness is a fulness of grace and I like to regard it as a participation in the life principle of the divinity, a supernatural life principle.

Every act of Christ on earth is a realization of this life, this new life Christ came to give you. When you act in full imitation of Christ, you share in this grace as Christ is now, the risen Christ, seated on his throne in heaven. But to do so, a great help is to know more and more deeply Christ's action while on earth, acting as Man, in order to give us the Word of *Life, Light and Love*—Father, Son and Holy Spirit!

Pray:

> *God our Father, your Son became man and was born of the*
> *Virgin Mary. May we become more like Jesus Christ whom*
> *I acknowledge as my redeemer, God and Man. "And the*
> *Word was made flesh and dwelt among us. And we saw his*
> *glory, glory as of the only begotten of the Father full of grace*
> *and truth".* (Jn 1:14).

As I said your real Director is the Holy Spirit. It is the Spirit of Love who will arouse in you the desire, the acceptance of and your personal correspondence with the Word of God, that is, the Gospel message. It is he who will be present to you during your retreat, presenting you with his genuine spiritual communication of the Word of God.

It is the Holy Spirit who will be present to you as you live your life of grace and practice the theological virtues of faith, hope and charity. He will be present in a special way in your prayer life, in your participation of the sacraments and sacramentals. He will act on our soul by means of movements which give light and energy and enable you to adapt to your present situation the meaning of the truths you are contemplating. It is the Holy Spirit which inspired the Word, the books of divine revelation and it is he who is the guarantor of the authenticity of the teachings of the Holy Church, the Mystical Body of Christ.

St. Ignatius says: "This is what I desire. Here it is to ask for an *intimate* knowledge of our Lord, who became man for me, that I may love him more and follow him more closely." By this intimate knowledge he means a person to person knowledge, not an abstract one. In this instance, Christ and you as a retreatant, are the persons and your spiritual knowledge will grow. You will get to know Christ more "intimately," with an ever increasing knowledge like that of his disciples. The Holy Spirit will inspire you with a spiritual knowledge through the theological virtues, above all through charity, in keeping with the Mystery of salvation, a Mystery of Love.

It is not a theoretical knowledge you seek but a practical one, for, as a result of your contemplation of Christ your Model, you will make your election. I would have you note that this does not require you to choose a vocation to the religious state but rather, in no matter what state of life you are now in, your choice must lead to a life of perfection out of love of Christ. There are married, single and religious saints!

The Mysteries Contemplated in the Second Week

I shall list the contemplations mentioned by St. Ignatius: the Annunciation to our Lady; the Visitation; the Birth of Christ; the Shepherds; the Circumcision; the Magi; the Purification of our Lady and the Presentation of the Child Jesus; the Flight into Egypt; the Return from Egypt; the Life of Christ from the age of Twelve to the age of Thirty; Jesus goes up to the Temple; the Baptism of Christ; the Temptation of Christ; the Vocation of the Apostles; the first Miracle at Cana; Christ casts the Sellers from the Temple; the Sermon on the Mount; Christ calms the Storm; Christ walks on the Waters; The Apostles sent to Preach; the The Conversion of Magdalene; Christ feeds five thousand; the Transfiguration; the Raising of Lazarus; Palm Sunday; Jesus preaches in the Temple.

Before I continue on this topic, pray!

> *God our Father, you have revealed the Mysteries of your*
> *Word through the Gospels. By prayer and reflection may I*
> *come to understand the wisdom they teach. Through the*
> *inspiration of the Holy Spirit. Amen.*

The very fact you will make the Ignatian Exercises, I hope, shows that you too want to live the *Following of Christ.* I, following St. Ignatius, introduced this Second Week with the contemplation on the Kingdom of Christ. Here is what Thomas A. Kempis says: "The Kingdom of God is within you, says the Lord (Lk 17:21). Turn then to God the Lord with your whole heart and forsake this wretched world, and your soul will find rest.

"Learn to despise what is outside of you and to give yourself over to what is within you, and you will come to know the Kingdom of God within you."

"For the Kingdom of God in us is peace and joy in the Holy Spirit (Rm 14:17) and this Kingdom is not for the unholy.

"O know that Christ comes to you and lets you enjoy his consolation, if you have prepared for him a worthy dwelling place within you.

"All his beauty and glory is from within, and therein is his delight.

"The inward man is whom he often visits. With him he loves to stay, conversing as friend to friend, giving him loving consolation, great peace, in such intimacy as makes both heaven and earth marvel" (*Following of Christ,* Bk II, Ch 1).

The Mysteries of the Hidden Life of Christ

Now, having begged for the grace to imitate Christ, you will "ponder in your heart"—imitating Mary—to Jesus through Mary— the events presented for meditation by St. Ignatius. Of course, you will not meditate during your retreat on everything that St. Ignatius proposes for a thirty day retreat. However, here is some advice on how you are to regard the events on which you do meditate. Though they are past events, you must be ever conscious that the persons involved exist for all eternity: the Divine Persons, the Blessed Mother, the angels, the saints, the disciples, Christ's friends and enemies, those who accepted and those who rejected him.

In keeping with this realization of persons present I suggest as a retreat and post-retreat practice, when, by the words of consecration Jesus is really present, no matter what distractions from outside the church or inside—organ or guitar music—prescinding from them, that you make yourself fully aware that he is really and truly present, as truly present as he was and is to his Father and the Holy Spirit— both also present—his mother, the apostles and the holy women.

When you receive him in Holy Communion, be not only aware of his presence but speak to him. Address him as "you." I assure you that the use of this word "you" will help you see, hear, touch and savor him. As Elizabeth said to Mary: "Who am I that the mother of my Lord should come to me?" So, say: "Who am I that *you* my Lord should come to *me*?"

St. Ignatius, in the distinction he makes between the events of Christ's hidden life and those of his public life, shows that God's ways are not our ways. To carry out his tremendous salvific work Jesus spends only three years, while he lived thirty years in apparent seclusion. I say "apparent", for every movement of his soul, every breath of his body, every thought of his mind was of salvific value in the eyes of his Father and of redemptive value for men.

Pray:

> *Jesus, Jesus, come to me! O how oft I sigh for thee! Welcome of all friends the best! Come and dwell within my breast! Comfort my poor soul distressed! Stay, o stay within my breast!*

The Incarnation: The Word of God Made Flesh

Before you begin meditating on the Incarnation I want to make a comparison so that you may realize its relevance and actuality for our times. St. Ignatius says that prior to the coming of Christ: "Those on the face of the earth, are in great diversity in dress and manner of acting. Some are white, some black; some at peace, and some at war; some weeping, some laughing; some well, some sick; some coming into the world, some dying; etc. Next, see how they speak to each other, swear and blaspheme etc., finally, see what they do, wound and kill. . ." (Ex. 106-108).

Compare this with what St. Paul says: "Do not forget this, there will be terrible times in the last days. Men will be lovers of self and of money, proud, arrogant, abusive, disobedient to their parents, brutal, hating the good. They will be treacherous, reckless, pompous, lovers of pleasure rather than of God as they make a pretense of religion but negate its power. Stay clear of them. It is such as these who work their way into homes and make captives of silly women burdened with sins and driven by desires of many kinds wanting to learn but never able to reach a knowledge of the truth. . ." (2 Tm 3:1-8).

St. Ignatius is not negative. Here is the positive side: "I will see the Three Divine Persons, our Lady and the Angel saluting her. I will hear the Divine Persons say: Let us work the redemption of the human race, the message of Gabriel, and Mary's answer. Finally, the Divine Persons work the most holy Incarnation, the Angel carries out his office of ambassador, and our Lady humbly consents" (Ex. 106-108).

Again compare this with what St. Paul says: "You for your part, must remain faithful to what you have learned and believed, because you know who your teachers were. Likewise, from your infancy you have known the sacred Scriptures, the source of the wisdom which through faith in Jesus Christ leads to salvation. . . (2 Tm. 3:9-17).

As you know St. Ignatius believed in repetition. I suggest you re-read this and make a further comparison. This time between what St. Paul says and what is going on today. There is found certainly what St. Ignatius calls the marks of Satan: pride and confusion! Now, of course, you can say piously—and I do too somewhat humorously: "Yeah, God alone knows what's going on!"

It can also be said about our fellow men who do not know the truth revealed by God that he will judge them according to their knowledge and sincerity. Yet even though this is true that, though man violates the objective law of God out of ignorance, he is still saved, this is no reason for you not to spread the truth, the Word of God! God knows full well that he will save the ignorant but despite this he sends his only begotten Son to bring men to the knowledge of his objective law, especially through his ever present Body, his Mystical Body, the Church.

This is why St. Ignatius, especially during this Second Week when you are meditating on the Mysteries of the Incarnate Word, wants you by word and example to bring as many of your fellow men as possible to the Church where they will be so greatly aided by the sacraments and sacramentals, the efficacious signs of grace, and endowed with the new life principle Christ came to bring you.

With this in mind, St. Ignatius presents to you the divine decree establishing the plan of salvation for fallen man. With divine foresight—humanly speaking—the Divine Persons behold the results of original sin. In their Eternity they decree that the Second Person become man to save the human race; the Word is to become Incarnate.

So when the fullness of time had come, they sent the Angel

Gabriel to Mary. This decree could have been carried out by sending the Word as omnipotent, omniscient regal Being, wholly endowed with the fully developed faculties of a genius. Instead he came as a babe in his mother's womb!

The Nativity: The Babe of Bethlehem

Remember! "Once in royal David's city stood a lowly cattle shed where a mother laid her baby in a manger for his bed. Mary was that mother mild, Jesus Christ her only child."

Pray:

> *God of love and mercy, help me to follow the example of Mary, always ready to do your will. At the message of an angel she became the temple of your Word, who lives and reigns with you and the Holy Spirit, one God, for ever and ever. "Blessed is the Virgin Mary who kept the word of God and pondered it in her heart"* (Lk 19).

God's ways are not our ways and so behold the Babe of Bethlehem— not Rome, not Athens! See him growing up in the obscure town of Nazareth, not known as the son of the Emperor of Rome or of the High Priest of Jerusalem but of Joseph, a carpenter. It was to a carpenter that the Lord of the universe was obedient: He went down with them, then, and came to Nazareth, and was obedient to them— Mary and Joseph (Lk 3:51)

Pray:

> *God our Father, in every age you call man to develop and use his gifts for the good of others. With St. Joseph as my example and my guide, help me to do the work you have asked and come to the rewards promised. Almighty God, you entrusted to the faithful care of Joseph the beginnings of the mysteries of man's salvation. Through his intercession may your Church always be faithful in her service so that your designs will be fulfilled.*

In these meditations and those of the rest of your retreat your spiritual director will follow this advice given you by St. Ignatius: "The one who explains to another the method of meditating should narrate accurately the facts. Let him adhere to the points, and add only a short summary explanation. "Why"? The reason for this is that when you, in meditating take the solid foundation of facts, and go over it and reflect on it for yourself, you may find something that makes them a little clearer or better understood. They may come either from your own reasoning, or from the grace of God enlightening the meaning at great length. Now this produces greater spiritual relish and fruit than if the one giving the Exercises had explained and developed the meaning at great length. For it is not much knowledge that fills and satisfies the soul, but the intimate understanding and relish of the truth. Listen, now, to St. Ignatius' favorite author:

Close Association With Jesus

"When Jesus is with you, everything is fine and pleasant. But when he is absent, everything is hard and bitter. If Jesus does not comfort you, all else is as nothing. But one word from his lips fills your heart with consolation. Did not Mary Magdalene rise immediately from where she was sitting weeping, as soon as Martha said: "The Master is come and calls for you?" What a happy hour for you when Jesus calls you from tears to spiritual joy" (Bk II, ch 8).

Jesus in His Father's House: the Temple

Holy Scripture tells you that "The Word became flesh and dwelt among us," man among men, like to man in all things, sin alone excepted. He is seen as an ordinary man in his hidden life with but few exceptions. One of these exceptions, a manifestation that Jesus of Nazareth is not an ordinary person, is found in the contemplation of the Child Jesus in the Temple.

By meditating on this and other manifestations of the Word

made flesh as God, Son of the Eternal Father, you will learn that his true nature is shown in Scripture even before he, by his words and deeds, his preaching and miracles, revealed himself. You will be ever ready unconditionally to follow him truly, and to imitate his living for so many years as "ordinary," by living after your retreat your ordinary life in closer and closer union with him.

Before you start your meditation you place yourself in the presence of God, having read or heard of the contents (Lk 2:41-51)— *The Finding in the Temple.* Do not forget to see the persons, places and things; hear the words spoken; sense and savor the entire scene which unrolls before your imagination; reflect and then, with your will resolve to do what God inspires you to do for his greater glory.

I say *hear* what Christ says. *See* what his blessed mother does. Then *resolve* to imitate them.

"Did you not know that I had to be about my Father's business? (Lk 2:49).

"His mother kept all these things carefully in her heart" (Lk 2:51). So, do likewise! Never forget to keep in your heart what you have learned on your retreat when you return home!

Pray:

> *Lord Jesus Christ in your person you joined humanity and divinity in an admirable union. In imitation of the Blessed Virgin Mary may I keep your word in all fidelity and preserve it throughout my life until you call me home for an eternal union.*

The Mysteries of the Public Life

St. Ignatius beautifully introduces you to these mysteries with a reference to our mother Mary. "After Christ our Lord had bidden farewell to his blessed Mother, he went from Nazareth to the River Jordan where St. John the Baptist was preaching."

In this period of the Second Week you will visit on your tour many places in the Holy Land. You will do so accompanied by Jesus. He will speak to you so listen to his words and when through his Holy Spirit he inspires you to make your *election*, your choice of the decisions and resolutions you will make, your heart will be filled with generosity to return love for love.

So now journey with him from Nazareth to the river Jordan where he is *baptized by John* and where the Holy Spirit descends on him and his Father's voice is heard saying: "This is my beloved Son in whom I am well pleased."

Pray:

> *Almighty and eternal God, when Christ was baptized in the Jordan and the Holy Spirit descended on him, you solemnly proclaimed him as your beloved Son. Grant to your sons by adoption, who were born again of water and the Spirit, that they may always persevere in pleasing you. "Happy are they who have kept the word with a generous heart, and yield a harvest through perseverance"* (Lk 18).

Then, go along with Jesus into the desert. In a sense, if you follow St. Ignatius' advice, on your retreat you will be with him in solitude (Ex. 20). There he fasted for forty days and was *tempted by the Master of Pride and Confusion.* When you are tempted, turn to him for help. He knows what it means for he is "like unto us in all things save sin."

Pray:

> *Father, you are filled with life and power while I am weak and in need. I beg you now and every day to fracture the power of sin in my life and to flood me with the light of your love who is Jesus. "I call upon you for you will answer me, O God. Incline your ear to me. Hear my words"* (Ps 17).

Then he calls his Apostles, as he is now calling you, to follow him and through this summons bring others to follow him. As he travels about, the Word brings the word of God to men. He helps others, works miracles, converts sinners, raises the dead and confirms his followers' faith in him as the Messiah.

In Imitation of Christ, pray!

> *Lord, you heal me in body and soul. You have called those*

> *who show mercy "blest" for mercy shall be theirs. Teach me to serve the poor and the needy with brotherly compassion that I may be received by you and always be with you. "Anyone who hears my words and puts them in practice is like the wise man who built his house on a rock" (Mt 7:24).*

I shall close these meditations on the public life of Christ by suggesting to you that when you attend the wedding feast at Cana where Christ worked his first miracle, you listen carefully and obey his mother's words: "Do whatever he tells you."

*Contemplations for the Choice of Greater Service of God
attend the wedding feast at Cana where Christ worked his first miracle, you listen carefully and obey his mother's words: "Do whatever he tells you."*

Contemplations for the Choice of Greater Service of God

Pray:

> *Almighty God, Father of our Lord Jesus Christ, faith in your word is the way to wisdom, and to ponder your divine plan is to grow in the truth. Open my eyes to your deeds, my ears to the sound of your call, so that every act may increase my sharing in the life you have offered me.*

The Ignatian Exercises present for your consideration the choice—election—of different states of life. St. Ignatius says: "The example which Christ our Lord gave of the first state of life, which is that of observing the Commandments, has already been considered in meditating on his obedience to his parents. The example of the second state, which is that of evangelical perfection, has also been considered, when he remained in the temple and left his foster father and mother to devote himself exclusively to the service of his eternal Father. *Whilst continuing to contemplate* his life, let us begin to investigate in what kind of life or in what state his Divine Majesty wishes to make use of us" (Ex. 135).

Again I want to point out that, when you make your retreat it is not necessary to make it in order to change your state of life. What you are to ask of the Holy Spirit is to help you ponder on how you have been serving and loving Christ in the life you are now leading whether it be lay or religious. While on retreat you may well, with the assistance of your director, be inspired to learn how you can more perfectly serve God within the same state of life in which you find yourself (Ex. 18).

Reformation of One's Way of Living in His State of Life

"Let him desire and seek nothing except the greater praise and glory of God our Lord as the aim of all he does. For every one must keep in mind that in all that concerns the spiritual life his progress will be in proportion to his surrender of self-love and of his own interests."

A Meditation on Two Standards: of Christ—of Lucifer

St. Ignatius warns you that one of the greatest dangers you as a human person face, though at the same time a great gift of God, is your free will. Your free will may be led astray by a deceitful being who, through pride and confusion, would have you imitate him instead of Christ.

You recall he even tempted Christ. Satan is a fallen archangel still endowed with an intelligence far superior to ours and a will to try to make you say with him to God: "I will not serve." He wants you to follow him as your leader under his standard and reject Christ and his standard.

Yet never forget that he can never force you to assent for you have that great gift of free will. Other creatures on the face of the earth give God material glory, that is, they do what their nature forces them to do. Man alone on the earth gives God formal glory. That is why God created him.

So offer up this prayer:

> *Almighty Father, strong is your justice and great is your*
> *mercy. Protect me in the burdens and challenges of life.*
> *Shield my mind from the distortion of pride and enfold my*
> *desire with the beauty of truth. Help me to become more*
> *aware of your loving design so that I may more willingly give*
> *my life in service to all. "Jesus looked up to heaven and*
> *prayed: O Father most holy, consecrate them by means of*
> *truth—your word is truth"* (Jn 17:17).

Though your free will has been threatened by the consequences of
original sin, with the help of God's grace—and that is why you should
make your retreat—your free will is strengthened to resist the assaults
of the Devil by the Christ who calls you to fight the Foe under his
standard. His Holy Spirit too will illumine your mind so that you will
be able to distinguish Satan's lies from Christ's words of truth,
especially those truths taught you by the Church against whom "the
Gates of hell shall not prevail!"

The Test of True Love

The true lover resists temptation, pays no heed to the suggestions
of his enemy the Devil. You know, the Devil, your foe of old, makes
every effort to obstruct your desire to do good, to lure you away from
any devout exercises. He inserts evil thoughts and desires into your
mind, to make you bored with prayer and spiritual reading. (As St.
Ignatius says, *agere contra*, that is, do not run away but stand up
against him! Tell him off!) Away from me, you traitor, you monster
of evil, you shall have no hold upon me. Jesus will be with me, like a
valiant warrior, and you will be defeated! (*The Following of Christ*,
Bk. III, "The Deceits of Satan").

Pray:

> *All-powerful Father, you have built your Church on the*
> *rock of Peter's confession of faith. May nothing divide or*
> *weaken our unity of faith and love.*

Reflect on this, especially today when those who hold that "God is love" deny the existence of sin, hell and evil spirits! I bring to your mind that one of the greatest fictional criminals is the *Invisible Man.* Satan is even greater in actuality. He has convinced many today that he does not exist, so he has become the "Non-existent Criminal." This, as I said before, leads not only to his being able to enter "idle minds" and make them his workshop, but into "empty minds" and make them his home!

This is an example of confusion due to the pride of some false shepherds. Remember! Empty your minds of temporal concerns and open it up and fill it with the Holy Spirit's divine truths. Having done this, then in this atmosphere of tranquil prayer, talk to God about your desire to overcome your sins, faults and negligences and to serve him and love him more perfectly.

Meditation on Three Classes of Men

I mentioned that one of the greatest dangers to your free will is Satan inspiring you with pride and confusion. There is, however, another danger much closer to you. It is the way you use your free will even though you may want to do something or not. This is what St. Ignatius presents here for your meditation.

The First Class. You may want to overcome something which you have come to realize is offensive to a friend of yours. But this "wanting" is a velleity, that is, you do not do anything to avoid offending him.

The Second Class. Your way of not offending him is not something he would want but which you prefer.

The Third Class. You not only do not want to offend him but you act toward him inoffensively even though it may inconvenience you.

So you see how in his *Spiritual Exercises*, St. Ignatius is a master of common sense. This friend is God and, as St. Ignatius says in the Third prelude: "beg for the grace to chose what is more for the glory of his Divine Majesty and the salvation of my soul." Here is a supreme instance of common sense!

Christ's Humility and Simplicity

St. Ignatius wants you to make the right choice so he presents you with an explanation of Christ's sign, the opposite of Satan's, namely *humility* and *simplicity*. Satan's slogan: "I will not serve!" Christ's: "One thing is necessary: do the will of my Father!" So as you meditate on what Jesus does and says in this phase of his life, keep ever in mind and strive to imitate in your later life his humility and simplicity. Be constantly aware of the *kenosis*: the Second Person of the blessed Trinity, the Only Begotten of the Father, the Word, the Sovereign Lord and Ruler of the universe. He became a man among men to bring us through the virtues of humility and simplicity to do the will of his Father and save our souls.

So you see you will now be living in Christ, with Christ and through Christ, living as he lived and living in him as other Christs live in him. Having chosen the way you are going to follow him, you are now to confirm that decision and do so by following him on the Way of the Cross. That will be the main topic of the Third Week of your Exercises.

A final prayer at the close of this Week.

> *Lord Jesus, gentle and humble of heart, you promised your kingdom to the humble and charitable. Never permit pride to rule my heart. Grant that I may accept your gentle yoke and obtain mercy and glory from your Father. (Humbly welcome the word that has taken root in you with power to save you)* (Jn 1:22).

Lernet von Mir, denn Ich bin sanftmüthig und demüthig von Herzen

Kommet alle zu Mir, die ihr mühselig und beladen seid Ich will euch erquicken

4

Chapter 5

THE PASCHAL MYSTERY: THE WAY OF THE CROSS

Introductory Prayer

> *God, through your Son in your Church you carried out your plan to redeem mankind from its ancient bondage and lead it to the heavenly land of promise by means of the paschal mystery, by your Word, sustain us on our pilgrimage that we may praise you for all eternity.*

In this phase of your retreat, the Third Week, you will ponder under the inspiration of the Holy Spirit the first stage of the Paschal Mystery and its dimension for your Christian life. In this Week you will contemplate the Passion of Christ, the mystery of the death of Christ. You will share with Christ his sorrows, for love is sharing.

The Plan of Salvation and the Paschal Mystery

The Old Testament prepared the way for Christ's coming to save Christ the Redeemer. The New Testament relates the accomplishment of our Savior's redemption. This salvation is applied in the Church through the sacraments and the word, the Gospel as inspired by the Holy Spirit and infallibly interpreted by the Church, and by means of Christian life based on faith and conversion.

You will see how, in the paschal mystery, the Father carries out his promises in Christ, saves us in Christ's death and resurrection, and how Christ, now glorified and seated at the right hand of the Father, sends his Spirit and continues his salvific work in the Church and in the world and will return as Judge and Savior.

St. Ignatius tells you, "consider how the divinity itself for example, could destroy its enemies and does not do so, but leaves the most sacred humanity to suffer so cruelly." Here too, is what Jesus Himself said to his disciple: "Put back your sword . . . Do you not suppose I can call on my Father to provide at a moment's notice more than twelve legions of angels?" (Mt 26:52). Then St. Ignatius adds: "consider the divinity, which seemed to hide itself during the Passion, now appearing and manifesting itself so miraculously in the most holy Resurrection in its true and most sacred effects" (Ex.223) Prepare a beautiful summary of the essence of each Week! This centricity of the divinity is the key to the paschal mystery as a single reality.

So pray this prayer which contains the essence of the whole Exercises: the plan of salvation fulfilled in the paschal mystery.

> *Father in the rising of your Son, death gives birth to new life.*
> *The suffering he endured restored hope to a fallen world.*
> *Let sin never ensnare me with empty promises of passing*
> *joy. Make me one with you always, so that my joy may be*
> *holy, and my love may give life.*

A Look Back on the Path Covered by Your Tour

This prayer should inspire you to review how you have thus far made the tour planned for you by St. Ignatius. Let us say that in the First Week, the Holy Spirit awakened in you a deeper awareness of your need for salvation and liberation, your need for that new life principle, grace which Christ brought. This was the first stage of your tour: reaching knowledge of self as a sinner, a slave thereby showing you the road away from or to God: following the false guide Satan or the true guide, the Holy Spirit, showing you Christ, the Way, the Truth and the Life.

Then came the Second Week, the following of that true Way to true Life through the Incarnate Word, a Word that calls you to know him more clearly, love him more dearly and follow him more nearly. During this Week, which presented you with a picture of Christ, man among man, like us in all save sin, the Holy Spirit inspired you to answer the summons of your King giving you a deepened experiential knowledge of what "the imitation" of Christ really means. This, under the form of the "election," enabled you to experience true liberation, a passing from a condition of servitude to the world, the flesh and the devil," to a condition of true freedom, a surrender of self-love and of your own will and interests to the greater glory of God.

So now, in the Third and Fourth Weeks, you come to the mystical meaning of "to die with him in order to live with him and for God" (Rm 5:8-11). St. Ignatius expresses this when he says: "It is my will to conquer the whole world and all my enemies, and thus to enter into the glory of my Father. Therefore, whoever wishes to join me in this enterprise, must be willing to labor with me, that by following me in *suffering* he may follow me in *glory*."

In the Third Week and in the Fourth Week you will contemplate the mysteries of the Passion and Resurrection as a single mystery: the divinity which hides itself during the Passion is the same divinity which manifests itself in the Resurrection and Ascension. These events do not remain external to you as a retreatant but penetrate and transform you in your innermost depths. You "consider that Christ suffers all this for my sins, and what I ought to do and ought to suffer for him," (Ex. 197). You are, then asked "to be glad and rejoice intensely because of the great joy and the great glory of Christ our Lord" (Ex. 221).

The Mysteries of the Third Week

I suggest that during this Week, that of the Passion and Death of Christ, you read the various accounts in the Gospels and make the Stations of the Cross.

> *Lord our God, you formed man from the clay of the earth and breathed into him the spirit of life, but he turned from your face and sinned. I call out for your mercy. Bring me*

*back to you and to the life your Son won for me by his death
on the cross.*

I shall now follow the sequence of the Exercises as St.
Ignatius presents them to you and let you know how you will be making his
Way of the Cross: the Last Supper; the Agony in the Garden; from
the house of Annas to that of Caiphas and to that of Pilate; from
Pilate to Herod and back to Pilate; Christ is condemned and dies on
the Cross and is buried.

The Meaning of the Third Week

The meaning of this week of the Exercises may be gleaned from
the Preludes to the various contemplations St. Ignatius proposes. I
shall quote just two. "This is to ask what I desire. Here it will be to ask
for sorrow, compassion and shame, because the Lord is going to his
suffering for my sins" (Ex. 103). "In the Passion it is proper to ask for
sorrow with Christ in sorrow, anguish with Christ in anguish, tears
and deep grief because of the great affliction Christ endures for me"
(Ex. 203). Incidently I would suggest you feel compassion for Mary
who stood at the foot of the Cross!

The key word is *compassion*, suffering along with, a sharing in
the paschal mystery, in the passion of Christ. This compassion is the
sorrow you will feel spiritually, affliction of soul, generous,
stimulating which comes from love, that love generated for Christ in
the Second Week, a love which creates within you an interior
disposition to "remove" what you saw in the First Week that kept you
apart from God. You want to be so close to Christ as to share his
Passion—suffer *with him—compassion.*

The Last Supper—Holy Eucharist

I suggest here that when you are present at Holy Mass and
receive Christ in Holy Communion you fill your mind with this
wondrous Gift God has given you to give to him who in return, not
being outdone in generosity, gives you that Gift back, the Body and

Blood, Soul and Divinity of Christ, his glorified Body still bearing the marks of his infinite love, the scars of the wounds on his hands, feet and side!

Pray:

> God our Father, I am in your Presence to share in the supper which your only Son left to his Church to reveal his love. He gave it to us to celebrate it as the new and eternal sacrifice. I pray that in this Eucharist I may find the fullness of love and life.

While you are in this spirit of compassion reflect that at the Last Supper that love was rejected as you have at times rejected it by sin. As St. Ignatius says: "He eats the Paschal Lamb with his disciples, to whom he predicts his death: 'Amen I say to you, one of you shall betray me.' When Judas had gone out to sell his Lord, Christ addressed his disciples."

My Lord, My God, My All!

> Who am I that you, my Lord and God should come to me?" So, then, my soul, be glad, and thank the Lord for this so wondrous gift and so quickening a grace which he has left behind for us in this vale of tears!

For as often as you gratefully ponder this Mystery and partake of the Body of Christ, so often will you share in Christ's merits, so often will you fulfill within you anew the work of salvation.

For the love of Christ is never lessened and the stream of his intercession, as his love, never runs dry!

Therefore you ought to prepare yourself each time for this Sacrament by pondering the great mystery of salvation. Whenever you say or attend Mass, it is to seem to you as wondrous, as marvellous and as joyous as if that same day Christ had first come down into the Virgin's womb and become man; as if he were nailed to the cross, suffering and dying for the salvation of men. *(The Following of Christ,* Bk. IV, 6).

To help you appreciate the *Real Presence* of Christ on the altar and within you when you receive Holy Communion, I shall quote what Pope Gregory VII, decreed in 1079 against Berengarius' denial of the Real Presence, a denial later repeated by Calvin and alas by some neo-theologians who deny *transubstantiation* and hold there is *transignification.* This means that at Mass the bread and wine merely take on a new meaning. Berengarius was ordered to recant by taking the following oath:

> *"I believe in my heart and profess with my lips that the bread and wine which are placed upon the altar are, by the mystery of the sacred prayer and words of the Redeemer, substantially changed into the true and life-giving flesh and blood of Jesus Christ our Lord; and that after the Consecration, there is present the true Body of Christ which was born of the Virgin and—offered for the salvation of the world—hung on the Cross and now sits at the right hand of the Father; and that there is present the true Blood of Christ which flowed from His side. They are present not only by means of a sign and of the efficacy of the sacrament, but also in the very reality and truth of their nature and substance."*
> (Denzinger 355).

I urge you to repeat wholeheartedly this testimonial of your very own belief!

Before passing on to the next mystery of Christ's Passion, I shall quote something very appropriate from St. Ignatius: "I will take care not to bring up pleasing thoughts, even though good and holy. Rather I will rouse myself to sorrow, suffering and anguish by frequently calling to mind the labors, fatigue and suffering which Christ our Lord endured from the time of his birth down to the mystery of the Passion upon which I am engaged at present" (Ex. 206).

Pray:

> *God, you left me a memorial of your passion in this wonderful sacrament. Make me revere the sacred mysteries of your body and blood so as constantly to enjoy the fruits of your redemption.*

The Agony in the Garden

When the Supper was finished . . . Jesus full of fear (a man like to you in all save sin), goes forth with his disciples to Mount Olivet. — Sorrow! "My soul is sorrowful even unto death." Yet, just as you should do in time of fear and sorrow, he prays: "My Father, if it be possible let this cup pass from me, yet not as I will but as *thou* willest." And falling into an agony he prayed the more earnestly. So, imitate Christ and pray!

> *Lord, grant your mercy to your faithful. You give food to those who fear you and will be ever mindful of your covenant. Strengthen my faith with your Word and nourish me in the sacrificial banquet.*

The Way of the Cross—from the Garden to Calvary

As you follow Christ from the Garden to Calvary use your God given faculties of memory, intellect and will, and especially use your faculty of *creative* imagination, the use of the five senses: see the blood flowing: hear his words: "Father, forgive them"; touch his wounds as did Thomas after the Resurrection; smell and taste the vinegar and gall! See, talk to, listen to his blessed Mother whose soul that sword foretold has pierced.

Recall these specific points: Judas, one of the chosen twelve kisses him in betrayal; Peter, restored later on to grace, denies him thrice; the mulitude shouts; Crucify him!" He prayed for those who crucified him; he pardoned the thief; he cried out "I thirst; he said he was forsaken; then, "It is consummated" and finally, "Father into thy hands I command my spirit."

With Peter, who denied him, his apostles who ran away and with the Good Thief, pray:

> *Lord, you brought me to the fountain of life, the tree planted near running waters. Grant that we may bear perpetual fruit through the cross of your Son and be admitted into the assembly of the just.*

The word of the Cross is folly to those who are perishing, but to us who are being saved it is the power of God. (1 Cor 1:18).

As you stand in contemplation before the cross, recall that: "Thou shalt call his name Jesus, for he shall save his people from their sins" (Mt 1:21). Jesus brings about in an unexpected way God's salvation. He accomplished it perfectly throughout his life but especially by his Passion and Death. He, man, takes on himself the consequences of sin and by his own death liberates this world. As God, he satisfies God's justice out of love. That is why, whether we speak of mercy or justice, when we speak of God, we speak of love, for God is Love.

Here is something I found in a *Monthly Leaflet of the Apostleship of Prayer*. You of course, are familiar with the glorious hymn to our Lady, the *Stabat Mater*: "At the cross her station keeping, stood the holy Mother weeping close to Jesus to the last." The leaflet continues: "Virgin of virgins blest! Listen to my fond request, Let me share thy grief divine. Let me to my latest breath, in my body bear the death of that dying Son of Thine."

Then you are addressed: The Triumph of the Cross.

"When you look at the crucifix, you see the terrible reality of man's inhumanity to man, and you realize that today, with all our talk of civilization, we are capable of similar barbarities, of abortions, killings, violence and hatred. The crucifix silently testified to eveil and sin and to our constant need of repentance. But it also testified to Christ's redemptive power and healing love. The hands nailed to the cross are welcoming hands; the bruised lips pray for forgiveness for the world; the pierced Heart is open to all.

"They shall look on him whom they pierced. If only you would look more often and more attentively! In deep repentance you would ask for forgiveness knowing that pardon and forgiving love are close at hand."

Pray to that pierced Heart, open to you and all men!

Sacred Heart of Jesus, open wide your heart broken by man's cruelty, that heart the symbol of love's triumph, the

pledge of all that man is called to be. Teach me to see you in the lives I touch, and to offer you living worship by love-filled service to my brothers and sisters.
Open our minds and our hearts to receive in our own day the word you speak to us in your Son, our Lord Jesus Christ.
(Lk 1; Heb 1:2).

The Interior Sufferings of Christ

During your retreat, from the very beginning you were drawn to Jesus. Now in this Week especially you are attracted to Jesus Crucified. In your contemplation of Jesus on the cross you "applied your senses," you "used the three powers of your soul," to feel his external pain, suffering and anguish. Yet another stage will teach you to appreciate his interior suffering as *Priest, Host, Victim*.

Just as the Third and Fourth Weeks cover but one single mystery, the paschal mystery, so the Last Supper and the Cross and the Resurrection are but another aspect of that one and the same mystery. In this mystery you will now contemplate Jesus as Priest and Host, Priest and Victim and later, in the Fourth Week you will contemplate the Risen Christ, whose sacrificial Gift of Self to his Father is accepted. Thus Christ is ever present in the Church through the Eucharist associating himself with all the members of his Mystical Body for continuing in each one and in you, by mystical incarnation, his mission of glorifying his Father and saving men.

Time and again you have been told you are to become "other Christs." Christ is like a prism the light from which is refracted in varied luminous rays suited to each one of his members. You must, on your retreat, try to reproduce Jesus in yourself through the transformation brought about by virtues, that is, by way of the Cross, which will make you most like him.

St. Thomas Aquinas tells you that the interior and redemptive sufferings of Christ's soul were incomparably more painful than the physical pain he underwent on Calvary. The intensity of the inner and hidden sufferings of Christ's soul, in view of the expiation of all the sins of men, is measured by his infinite love. (III, 46, 6, 4).

These interior sufferings of the Heart of Jesus are sufferings undegone from his Incarnation to the Cross, inner sufferings of his soul in his inner Crucifixion and prolonged in the Eucharist. Man's unfaithfulness, ingratitude and rejection still cause this suffering. In heaven, as God, he cannot suffer. So, to find his Cross, he descended into this world and became Man. As God-Man he could infinitely suffer and thus pay the price of the salvation of so many souls. During his life on earth, he never desired anything except the Cross, and ever the Cross, wanting to show the world what is the sole wealth and happiness on earth, the currency which alone will buy eternal happiness.

These interior sufferings never left him for a single moment throughout the thirty-three years of his life on earth. These sufferings were hidden until Calvary. He smiled, he toiled, and only his Mother was aware and pondered in her heart when the sword would pierce her heart, the sword made concrete by the nailing of her Son to the Cross!

Pray:

> *Lord Jesus Christ, formidable is your power and wonderful is your holiness! By your Cross you have destroyed the sting of death. Enlighten and strengthen all who suffer that they may sing your praise forever.*
>
> *God, you are the source of holiness. Strengthen the priests and faithful of your Church and enlighten them by your word. Sanctify them through the blood of your Son and lead all men into your eternal splendor.*
>
> *Father, it was your will that the compassionate Mother of your Son should stand near the cross on which he was glorified. Grant that your Church, having shared in Christ's Passion may also participate in his Resurrection.*

Then, close this Week with this beautiful hymn to the Mother of Sorrows!

Stabat Mater

> *By the Cross her vigil keeping, stands the mournful Mother*

weeping; near her Son until the end.
Through her heart a sword is driven, and her soul to anguish
given, more than we can comprehend.
Who can contemplate God's Mother, at the feet of Christ,
our Brother, and no sympathy express?
Who can see her so afflicted by the wounds our sins inflicted,
and not share in her distress?
She beholds his desolation, for the sins of his own nation,
dying as a common thief.
In her soul she feels those bruises, every drop of blood
he loses, yet she cannot give relief.
Mother, let us share thy sorrow, from thy heart may we each
borrow love for Jesus crucified.

The Royal Road of the Holy Cross

Jesus, then said to his disciples: "If a man wishes to come after me, he must deny his very self, take up his cross, and begin to follow in my footsteps" (Mt 16:24). This seems to many a hard saying, yet how much harder will it be to hear what he will say at the Last Judgment: "Out of my sight, you condemned, into that everlasting fire prepared for the devil and his angels" (Mt 25:41). Those who now willingly hear and follow the word of the Cross, will not fear upon hearing the sentence of everlasting damnation. For,"Then the sign of the Son of Man will appear in the sky when the Lord shall come to judge us. Then all the servants of the Cross, who during their lives conformed themselves unto Christ crucified, will approach Christ the Judge with great confidence. Why, then are you afraid to take up the Cross which is your road to the kingdom of Christ?" (*The Following of Christ*, Bk. II, 1).

Chapter 6

THE PASCHAL MYSTERY: FOURTH WEEK:—CHRIST GLORIFIED

Introductory Prayer

God, who can fathom the mystery of your love? You gave your Son the cup of death to drink but did not let your holy one see corruption and brought him to heavenly glory. Grant that I may seek happiness in you alone and attain the fullness of joys in your presence in the glory of the Resurrection. The Word of God became man. We have seen his glory. (Jn 1:14).

The meaning of the Fourth Week

You, in the Fourth Week, will enter into the joy of the Lord, rejoicing with him risen, living and glorious. You will fill your mind with the thought of his great love still manifested in his glorified Body which bears the marks of his crucifixion now the Cross is a standard of Triumph!

Here are St. Ignatius' instructions on how you are to contemplate the mysteries of Christ's glorification. "Ask for the grace to be glad and rejoice intensely because of the great joy and the glory of Christ our Lord". "Strive to feel joy and happiness at the great joy and happiness of Christ our Lord." "Consider the office of consoler that Christ our Lord exercises, and compare it with the way in which

friends are wont to console each other." This is to be applied to the contemplations you make on those whom he revealed himself to after his Resurrection and to his Ascension when he commanded them to await the coming of the Holy Spirit.

The apparition of Christ our Lord to our Lady

"After Christ expired on the cross his body remained separated from the soul, but always united with the divinity. His soul, likewise united with the divinity, descended into hell. There he set free the souls of the just, then came to the sepulcher, and rising, appeared in body and soul to his Blessed Mother," (Ex. 219).

> *Father, in your plan of salvation your Son Jesus Christ freed me from the power of the enemy. May I come to share the glory of his Resurrection. "This Son is the reflection of the Father's glory, the exact representation of the Father's being and he sustains all things by his powerful word"* (Heb 1:3).

Especially do I like to bring to your attention that St. Ignatius' first contemplation in this Fourth Week is Christ's apparition to his Mother. It is so revelatory of his devotion to our Lady and also of his common sense! He makes this comment: "He appeared to the Virgin Mary." Though this is not mentioned explicitly in the Scripture it must be considered as stated when Scripture says he appeared to many others. *For Scripture supposes we have understanding* (common sense), as it is written: "Are you too without understanding?" (Ex. 299). It is so logical that Christ would have appeared to his own Mother, she who "stood weeping at the foot of the Cross!" As she shared in his sorrow, now she shared in his joy!

Some say, if Jesus appeared to her first, why did she not tell the apostles and the holy women about it? I suggest they read what is said of Christ's Transfiguration: "he strictly enjoined them not to tell anyone what they had seen, before the Son of Man had risen from the dead (Mk 9:9). So it is likely he told his Mother something similar and of course, she "consented!"

As to the subsequent contemplations on Jesus Christ appearing after his Resurrection, here is what St. Ignatius has to say to help you really savor this phase of your retreat.

"In the subsequent contemplations, all the mysteries from the Resurrection to the Ascension inclusive are to be gone through in this manner: the first contemplation will serve as a guide; strive to feel joy and happiness at the great joy and happiness of Christ our Lord; call to mind and think on what causes pleasure, happiness and spiritual joy, for instance, the glory of heaven; make use of the light and the pleasures of the seasons, that it might help you rejoice in our Creator and Redeemer."

I would also have you reflect on the fact that the apparitions of Christ after he had risen from the tomb give us another instance of the truth that God's ways are not our ways. Just go over the list of those to whom he appeared: Mary his Mother, Mary Magdalene, the holy women, the apostles and disciples and many of his followers among the people. But he did not, as would have been expected of a mere man—a God-Man's ways are not a mere man's ways—appear in the splendor of his glorified Body before Pilate, Herod, not even in the temple before Annas and Caiphas! Apply this lesson to your life today! The great leaders of the world, in all areas, some in science, literature, art, education, politics and even in religion reject his Mystical Body, the Church, even persecute it! But, as I said, he concerned but never anxious! God knows what is going on, so conform your will to his. This is not the first era in which he has suffered in this world though, in heaven, he no longer can.

So Pray!

> *Lord our God, all truth is from you, and you alone bring oneness of heart. Give our people the joy of hearing your word in every sound and of longing for your presence more than life itself. May all the attractions of a changing world serve only to bring us the peace of your kingdom which this world cannot give. This is He who came in water and in blood—Jesus Christ. There are three that bear witness in heaven: the Father, the Word and the Holy Spirit, and these*

three are one, and these are three that bear witness on earth: the spirit, the water and the blood, and these three are one.

Hear now what the Word, the Word made flesh, said to Thomas: "You became a believer because you saw me. Blest are they who have not seen and have believed." (Jn 20:29).

The Effects of the Resurrection

St. Ignatius advises you: "consider the divinity . . . now appearing and manifesting itself so miraculously in the most holy Resurrection in its *true and most sacred effects"* (Ex. 223).

These sacred effects show you that Christ's death is not an end but a beginning. It is the beginning of a new "life"—the bestowing on man of the image in which he is created, the image of God. I say it is the beginning for the cause came in the days of Christ, but the effects, as I said before, refer back to the sin of our First Parents, a sin forgiven by the merits of Christ's death and Resurrection by *anticipation.* Again we are dealing with the Eternal Now! Through his death and resurrection man thereby, through adoption, becomes a partaker in the divinity of God—brothers in Christ as brothers of Christ! The life principle of this new life is Jesus, risen, living, glorified!

Hear what the Word, Christ tells you! "I am the light of the world. No follower of mine shall ever walk in darkness; no, he shall possess the light of life" (Jn 8:12). I am the resurrection and the life. Whoever believes in me, though he should die, will come to life and whoever is alive and believes in me will never die" (Jn 11:25-26).

You will recall that in the contemplation on the Kingdom, Christ told you: "It is my will to conquer the whole world and all my enemies, and thus enter into the *glory* of my Father. Therefore, whoever wishes to join me in this enterprise must be willing to labor with me, that by following me in suffering, he may follow me in glory. "Christ's triumph is not only as an individual but also social. Today especially when social justice is of such importance, this sacred effect is one you should implore will be fulfilled in you.

Pray:

> *God, rescuer of the afflicted and the needy from their despoilers. You came to the aid of your Son against those who oppressed him without cause. Help the Church in her earthly pilgrimage toward you that the weak and afflicted may take strength and their tongues tell of your justice.*

You have the great privilege of living with, in and through one of the effects of the Resurrection: the *Risen Christ—Priest and Victim.*

Christ is Priest and Victim, the Host immolated on the Cross, now Risen and perpetuated in the state of Victim—his Body, Blood, Soul and Divinity Really Present, still bearing the marks of his infinite love, the scars of the wounds on his hands, and feet and side— victim till the end of time to the glory of the Father and the salvation of the world.

In the Church, his Mystical Body, of which you are a member, the supreme form of her devotion to her Lord and Savior, her High Priest and Holocaust is the eucharistic sacrifice. This is not merely a symbol but the efficacious sign, the memorial which renders him really present in his pilgrim and militant Church. The Risen Christ, with his Personality of the Word, inseparable from the Trinity, holds himself day and night raised above the earth between God and man for the glory of the Trinity and the salvation of the world.

Listen to the words of the Word: "I am the way, the truth and the life . . . whoever has seen me has seen the Father. . . . Believe me that I am in the Father and the Father is in me . . . On that day you will know that I am in my Father, and you in me, and I in you" (Jn 5:9, 11, 20).

Christ is glorified, ever present before the face of the Father, in the bosom of his Church triumphant, the same Christ who once travelled—with no place to rest his head—along the roads of Samaria, of Judea, of Galilee. The same Christ born of the Virgin Mary, the true Christ of history, the unique Christ, is ever here among us. Hidden under the appearance of the Host and the Chalice of his Blood, there is the Presence of the highest divine reality, the authentic Presence of the Eternal Incarnate Word, binding together earth and heaven, the cosmos and the Trinity.

Jesus, the Incarnate Crucified Word, who by his interior sufferings even more than by his external Passion, saved us by the

Cross, as Priest and Host leaves to his Church an efficacious memorial of his Real Presence and of his ceaseless action on each one of us until the end of time, until the "consummation" of men in unity with the Father, the Son and the Holy Spirit. The Trinity is the beginning and the end of this economy of salvation, but Christ— Mediator through his royal Priesthood, shared by his own, constitutes the keystone of his mission of bringing glory to his Father and saving men.

I suggest you read carefully and prayerfully what Vatican II says about this "royal Priesthood" in which you share:

"Christ the Lord, High Priest taken from among men, made a kingdom to God his Father out of this new people. The baptized, by regeneration and the anointing of the Holy Spirit, are consecrated into a spiritual house and a *holy priesthood*. Thus through all these works befitting Christian men they can offer *spiritual sacrifices* and proclaim the power of him who has called them out of darkness into his marvellous light. Therefore *all* the disciples of Christ, persevering in prayer and praising God should present themselves as living sacrifices, holy and pleasing to God. Everywhere on earth they must bear witness to Christ and give an answer to those who seek an account of that hope of eternal life which is in them."

The Council continues making clear the distinction between ordained priests and the laity, so relevant today.

"Though they differ from one another *in essence and not only in degree,* the common priesthood of the faithful and the ministerial or hierarchical priesthood are nonetheless interrelated. Each of them in its own essential way is a participation in the one priesthood of Christ. The ministerial priest, by the sacred power he enjoys, molds and rules the priestly people. Acting in the person of Christ, he brings about the Eucharistic Sacrifice, and offers it to God in the name of all the people. For their part, the faithful join the offering of the Eucharist by virtue of their royal priesthood by receiving the sacraments, by prayer and thanksgiving, by the witness of a holy life, and by self-denial and active charity" *(Lumen gentium).*

The Ascension of Christ

You will recall how humanly and humanely Christ acted toward the sister of Martha and of Lazarus before and after his Resurrection. Mary had surely chosen the better part. Listen to what he tells her as she cries out "Rabboni" and clings to his feet. "Do not cling to me for I have not yet ascended to the Father. Rather, go to my brothers and tell them: "I am ascending to my Father and your Father, to my God and your God" (Jn 21:17).

Pray:

> *Lord Jesus, King of the universe, you let me feast joyfully at your sacred banquet. Help your flock to understand death that we may proclaim your triumph over death and your Ascension to the right hand of your Father.*

This is the last contemplation of the Fourth Week in the *Spiritual Exercises.* However, after I tell you what the Scripture, the word of God, tells you about the Ascension, I shall close this Week with the following contemplation:

The eleven disciples made their way to Galilee, to the mountain to which Jesus had summoned them . . . Jesus came forward and addressed them in these words:

> *"Full authority has been given to me both in heaven and on earth; go, therefore, and make disciples of all the nations. Baptize them in the name of the Father, and of the Son, and of the Holy Spirit. Teach them to carry out everything I have commanded you. And know that I am with you always, until the end of the world.* (Mt 28:16-20).
>
> *"Then, after speaking to them the Lord Jesus was taken up into heaven and took his seat at God's right hand"* (Mk 16:19).
>
> *"Then he led them out near Bethany, and with hands upraised, blessed them. As he blessed, he left them and was taken up into heaven"* (Lk 24:50-51).
>
> *"You will receive power when the Holy Spirit comes*

down on you; then you are to be my witnesses... even to the ends of the earth. No sooner had he said this than he was lifted up before their eyes in a cloud which took him from their sight. They were still gazing up into the heavens when two men dressed in white stood beside them: 'men of Galilee,' they said, 'why do you stand here looking up at the skies? This Jesus who has been taken from you will return just as you saw him go up into the heavens' " (Ac 1:8-11).

When you contemplate Christ rising up into heaven in this stage of your retreat, renew in the light of his Passion and Resurrection the resolutions, the Holy Spirit inspired you to make and will help you to carry out when you return to your daily life.

The Descent of the Holy Spirit

There are some who say that until our days the Holy Spirit was the unknown Person of the Holy Trinity. Everyone knew the Father and the Son but how much thought or prayer was directed to the Holy Spirit? Personally, from my own experience—way back in my childhood in catechism classes taught by nuns,—the Sisters of Charity—I recall being made conscious of the Presence of the Holy Ghost. He was really and truly present as the Father and the Son. We were not only taught how to make the Sign of the Cross and also the *Glory be to the Father, the Son and the Holy Ghost* . . . but I still remember the beautiful hymns, such as, "Come Holy Ghost, Creator blest and in our hearts take up thy rest, come with thy grace and heavenly aid to fill the hearts which thou *has made!"* I also remember "Come Holy Ghost, replenish the hearts of the faithful and grant us in your same Holy Spirit to relish what is right and just and ever rejoice in your consolations.

Besides, when we were taught Biblical History in grammar school we saw the Holy Ghost as a dove, as a flame etc. So listen to what the Word—Light, sent down to us by his Father—Life, has to tell you about his Spirit—Love!

Here is what the Holy Ghost tells us about himself in the Scripture he inspired.

Mary said to the angel: "How can this be since I do not know man? The angel answered her: "The Holy Spirit will come upon you and the power of the Most High shall overshadow you; hence, the holy offspring to be born will be called Son of God" (Lk 1:34-35).

"Now this is how the birth of Jesus Christ came about. When his mother Mary was engaged to Joseph, she was found with child through the power of the Holy Spirit . . . The angel of the Lord appeared: "Joseph, son of David, have no fear about taking Mary as your wife. It is by the Holy Spirit *she has conceived this child"* (Mt 18-20).

When Elizabeth heard Mary's greeting, the baby leaped in her womb. Elizabeth was filled with the Holy Spirit *. . .* (Lk 1:41). *Then Zechariah his father (John the Baptist's) filled with the* Holy Spirit, *uttered this prophecy.* (Lk 1:67). (The Canticle of Zechariah).

John answered them all by saying: "I am baptizing you in water, but there is one to come who is mightier than I and I am not fit to loosen his sandal strap. He will baptize you in the Holy Spirit *and in fire." (Lk 3:16).*

John gave this testimony also: "I saw the Spirit *descend like a dove from the sky, and it came to rest on him. But I did not recognize him. The one who sent me to baptize with water told me: "When you see the* Spirit *descend and rest on someone it is he who is to baptize with the* Holy Spirit. *Now I have seen for myself and have testified:" "This is God's chosen One."* (Jn 1:31-34).

At that moment Jesus rejoiced in the Holy Spirit *and said: "I offer you praise, of Father, Lord of heaven and earth . . ."* (Lk 10:21). *Suddenly, from up in the sky there came a noise like a strong, driving wind which was heard all through the house where they were seated. Tongues as of fire appeared on each of them. All were filled with the Holy Spirit.* (Ac 2:1-3).

This is what the Scripture inspired by the Holy Spirit, tells us about himself. This is what Jesus himself tells us about the Holy Spirit!

Luke tells us what Jesus revealed about the Holy Spirit. Listen to the words of the Word of God!

"If you, with all your sins, know how to give your children good things, how much more will the heavenly Father give the *Holy Spirit* to those who ask for him" (Lk 13).

"Anyone who speaks against the Son of Man will be forgiven but whosoever blasphemes the *Holy Spirit* will never be forgiven. When they bring you before synagogues, rulers and authorities, do not worry about how to defend yourselves or what to say. The *Holy Spirit* will teach you at that moment all that should be said" (Lk 12:10-12).

John was known as the Apostle whom Jesus loved. Love, as we have seen, is the Holy Spirit. Here is what John says Jesus said about the Holy Spirit.

> *Jesus replied (to Nicodemus): "I solemnly assure you, no one can enter into God's kingdom without being begotten by water and* Spirit. *Flesh begets flesh,* Spirit *begets spirit. Do not be surprised that I tell you, you must be begotten from above. . . "* (Jn 3:4-7).

To the Samaritan woman Jesus said: "Yet an hour is coming, and already is here, when authentic worshippers will worship the Father in *Spirit* and truth. Indeed, it is just such worshippers the Father seeks. God is Spirit and those who worship him must worship him in *Spirit* and truth" (Jn 4:23-24). "I will ask the Father and he will give you another Paraclete—to be with you always: the *Spirit* of truth the world cannot accept, since it neither sees him nor recognizes him . . . " (Jn 14:16-17). "The Paraclete; the *Holy Spirit* whom the Father will send in my name, will instruct you in everything, and remind you of all that I told you" (Jn 14:26).

"I have much more to tell you, but you cannot bear it now. When he comes, however, being the *Spirit* of truth he will guide you to all truth, *He will not speak on his own* but will speak only what he hears, and will announce to you the things to come. In doing this he will give glory to me, because he will have received from me what he will announce to you . . . " (Jn 16:12-15). You will recall I mentioned before that some false shepherds are confusing the faithful by teaching that we are now in the era of the Holy Spirit and that Christ's era is passé!

Then he breathed on them and said: "Receive the *Holy Spirit*. If you forgive men's sins they are forgiven them; if you hold them bound, they are held bound" (Jn 20:23).

Before we pass on to the final chapter on the *Contemplation to Attain Divine Love*, I suggest you read over those words spoken by the Word himself, using the Third Method of Prayer of the *Spiritual Exercises*, (Ex. 258) a measured rhythmical recitation, directing the attention to the meaning of the word, the Person, the Word, addressed. Next, read over carefully and prayerfully the text of the Descent of the Holy Spirit (Ac 2). Finally, recall what I said about the Father being Life—the Son Light—and the Holy Spirit Love. Even though all are equally Life, Light and Love, at the close of your retreat call on the Holy Spirit to fulfill his promise to you filling you with the gifts of Life, Light and Love!

Close with these prayers!

> *Merciful God, grant that your Church, assembled in the Holy Spirit, may be wholly devoted to you, and all her members united in purity of will.*
> *"Shine on the world like bright stars, you are offering it the word of life." (Ph 2:15, 16).*
> *Father, you sent your Word to bring me truth and your Spirit to make me holy. Through them I come to know the mystery of your life. Help me to worship you; one God in three Persons, by proclaiming and living my faith in you. He who keeps the word of Christ grows perfect in the love of God* (1 Jn 2:5).

Chapter 7

THE CROWN OF THE EXERCISES: GOD IS LOVE

Pray:

I want to be strong enough, Father, to love you above all and our brothers and sisters because of you. Help me with the power of your unbounded love.

Reflect:

Beloved, let us love one another because love is of God; everyone who loves is begotten of God and has knowledge of God. The man without love has known nothing of God, for God is love (1 Jn 4:7-8).

When you make this *Contemplation to attain the love of God* (Ex 230-237), it signals you *have reached your destination*, you are to disembark! On your tour you have come closer to God, Father, Son and Holy Spirit and are to begin your flight home, and resume your ordinary daily routine. This Contemplation is a compendium of the fresh view of the world you have received, Light, and a new surge of Life. So from now on you are going to keep in mind, with the help of the souvenirs you have received, the special graces you have been given to help you keep the resolutions you made inspired by the Holy Spirit, Love. This Contemplation will give you the supreme motive to do so: Love, love of God who is love.

Throughout your retreat you were conscious of the Presence of Jesus Christ, God-Man. Here, too, Christ is present to you but the stress is on his *oneness*—on his *eternal Now*—His existence before the beginning of time—his *divinity*.

Listen prayerfully to what the Word made Flesh says about this! They pressed him. "And where is this *Father* of yours?" Jesus replied, "You know neither me nor my Father. If you knew me, you would know my Father too" (Jn 8:19).

"You belong to what is below, I belong to what is above. You belong to this world—a world which cannot hold me. That is why I said you would die in your sins. You will surely die in your sins unless you come to believe that I AM" (Jn 8:23-24). Jesus continued, "When you lift up the Son of Man, you will come to realize that I AM" (Jn 8:28). "I solemnly declare it, Before Abraham came to be, I AM" (Jn 8:58).

Now, listen to your Director of the retreat you are making, St. Ignatius. Note, this time I do not say, if or when, or should you make a retreat. I want to bring out something I have hidden up to this moment, namely that if you have read carefully and prayerfully these instructions on the Word of God to know God, you have made a retreat! (Cf. Ex. 19). Here is the approach St. Ignatius would have you take toward the transcendent God of the *Principle and Foundation,* stressing his immanence along with the points of oneness, eternity and divinity.

He tells you to direct your mind and speak in the presence of *God Our Lord*—no distinction of persons; the *Divine Majesty*—in the presence of his angels and saints. Then he tells you to ask for an intimate knowledge of the blessings received—from the Father, the Son and the Holy Spirit, so that in gratitude you give him and yourself in return. Next, reflect on God's immanence in plants, animals and man. How he *created* you in his image and likeness; how he *conserves* what he has created by working and laboring in them. Finally, consider all blessings as a gift from the supreme and infinite power above. You may remember that I mentioned that St. Ignatius suggested you say a certain prayer at the end of your retreat which I urged you to recite at the end of Chapter I. So, now I urge you to follow his advice, turn back to that page and recite the prayer, *Take, Lord, and receive.*

In this Contemplation, St. Ignatius imparts to you a summary of what in every way and in everything corresponds to his view of the world and of living, a view dominated by God, a life lived for the greater glory of God. To bring this out more clearly, I shall make a comparison between this *Contemplation* and the *Foundation*. The *Foundation* presented you with a short theological summary. Your intellect played a major role in your consideration of your place in the world and before God. The *Contemplation*, however, is presented as an appeal to your sensitive spiritual faculty, particularly your visual and affective faculty. The grace you are to ask for is the gift by which God's word and deeds are seen clearly as coming from him, a gift of "seeing God in all things." The transition from that stage of "understanding" to the present stage of "appreciation" and "savoring" you have experienced as a gift from a loving God. You have not only learned about the "wonders" of your tour, but you have "seen" and "felt," "heard" and "smelled" and "savored" the immanence of God. God is not only the sovereign Being who created from without and rules, but God is the lover who is in and works within you, though still God who is infinite Majesty, omnipotent, omniscient and omnipresent.

Finally, recall the expression found in the *Foundation* known as the "magis," that is, your one desire and choice should be what is *more conducive* to the end for which we are created. This is explained in the *Contemplation* as "loving and serving in all things the Divine Majesty." So, at the end of your retreat you have learned that God's love is the goal of your tour. The tour is teaching you to overcome inordinate attachments and to endeavor to learn God's will. This is the road to love. You have before you one only "way": the imitation of God on an existential path of love.

You have learned that, as St. Ignatius says, "love is sharing." He also speaks of the "many blessings received." Now we know that God will not be outdone in generosity and that when, at the end of your retreat you offer yourself to his love and service, he will return gift for gift in infinite fold. But the question you must ask yourself is this: "In return for the many blessings I have received, will I though finitely, filled with gratitude for all, in all things love and serve the Divine Majesty?"

A Prayer for Love

Lord, open up my heart yet more and fill it with love, that my innermost being may savor how sweet it is to love and to flow in love and be immersed in the sea of love!

Let love hold me fast, as in unwonted fervor and wonder, I rise above myself.

Teach me the song of love, and let me follow thee, my Beloved, to highest heaven; let me, rejoicing in your love, pour myself out in praise of you!

Let me love thee more than myself and love myself out of love for thee; let me love of thee all who love thee, as the Law of love commands, that law whose light shines out from thee!

(The Following of Christ
Book III, Ch. 6)

Close with this prayer!

God, before all ages you are. You give me days and years that I may gain wisdom of heart. Make me submit to your love and discern in all creatures the traces of your generous hands until the day I shall contemplate you.

All that I am has been your gift to me, Lord. From my lips, with my heart, and in my very life I praise you, and we pray that whatever I do may be dedicated to you. Guide me, Father, in what I am about to do and help me in doing it; so that it may begin and come to an end in Jesus' name.

Father, give me your powerful light so that I will know your law of love and try to live it with open heart and open mind now, always and forever and ever!

Back to your normal daily life, ponder in your heart these closing words of the Word made Flesh:

"I am the true vine and my Father is the vinegrower. He prunes away every barren branch, but the fruitful ones he

trims clean to increase their yield. You are clean already, thanks to the word I have spoken to you. Live on in me, as I do in you. No more than a branch can bear fruit of itself apart from the vine, can you bear fruit apart from me. I am the vine, you are the branches. He who lives in me and I in him, will produce abundantly, for apart from me you can do nothing." (Jn 15:1-5).

IMMACULATE
CONCEPTION
CONVENT